D1631547

LUXURY STRATEGY IN ACTION

LUXURY STRATEGY IN ACTION

Edited by

Jonas Hoffmann

Associate Professor of Marketing, SKEMA Business School, France

and

Ivan Coste-Manière

Professor of Marketing, SKEMA Business School, France

palgrave
macmillan

First published 2012 by
PALGRAVE MACMILLAN

Palgrave Macmillan in the UK is an imprint of Macmillan Publishers Limited,
registered in England, company number 785998, of Houndmills, Basingstoke,
Hampshire RG21 6XS.

Palgrave Macmillan in the US is a division of St Martin's Press LLC,
175 Fifth Avenue, New York, NY 10010.

Palgrave Macmillan is the global academic imprint of the above companies
and has companies and representatives throughout the world.

Palgrave® and Macmillan® are registered trademarks in the United States,
the United Kingdom, Europe and other countries.

ISBN 978–0–230–35454–8

This book is printed on paper suitable for recycling and made from fully
managed and sustained forest sources. Logging, pulping and manufacturing
processes are expected to conform to the environmental regulations of the
country of origin.

A catalogue record for this book is available from the British Library.

A catalog record for this book is available from the Library of Congress.

10   9   8   7   6   5   4   3   2   1
21   20   19   18   17   16   15   14   13   12

Printed and bound in Great Britain by
CPI Antony Rowe, Chippenham and Eastbourne

CONTENTS

CONTENTS

6   INTERNET, SOCIAL MEDIA AND LUXURY STRATEGY   108
Fleur Gastaldi

7   BRANDING PRINCIPLES IN THE LUXURY INDUSTRY   125
Tinne Van Gorp

CONTENTS

CONTENTS

FIGURES AND CHARTS

Figures

TABLES

NOTES ON CONTRIBUTORS

Ivan Coste-Manière holds a doctorate in chemistry. He has extensive experience in the luxury industry and has created eight companies dealing with advertising, cosmetics, luxury goods and health care. He is currently Professor of Marketing at SKEMA Business School, Head of the Marketing Department and Director of the Master of Science in Luxury and Fashion Management.

Fleur Gastaldi post-graduated from SKEMA's Business School in 2005. Fleur is a young professional and a fulfilled web marketing and e-commerce manager whose professional perspective was initially enriched with an international relations and political sciences diploma.

Francesco Giliberti Birindelli studied law and economics at the Catholic University of Milan. He is a founder of [Trust] Partners, a multinational advisory firm and has been responsible for managing the worldwide taxes of the Gucci Group since 2006. He has also been Vice-President of the Supervisory Board of Marbert since 2010.

Betina Hoffmann holds an MSc in marketing. She is currently Business Development Manager of a cosmetics company in Monaco. She has previous experience in marketing and strategy in the luxury, fashion and cosmetics industry in Brazil and in France.

Jonas Hoffmann holds a doctorate in marketing from the University of Grenoble, France. He is currently Associate Professor of Marketing at SKEMA Business School. He has extensive experience in consulting and executive training and has written several articles about marketing, innovation and the luxury industry.

Jacques Molas has extensive experience in the luxury industry. He has managed from creativity till promotion all the various steps luxury products have to follow. Today, familiar with the worldwide distribution, he is currently acting as a project consultant and is involved in some important challenges.

Katrina Panchout holds a specialized masters in strategic communications management. She is Professor of Marketing at SKEMA Business School and Director of the International Master in Management Programme. She has extensive professional experience, having worked for companies such as Lacoste, Habitat and Weber Shandwick in France and England.

Giulio Pizzini manages EMEA Pricing for Georgia-Pacific, a consumer goods and industrial company. He holds a degree in computer engineering from Politecnico di Milano and an MBA from Harvard Business School.

Alessandro Quintavalle graduated in management and economics engineering at Politecnico di Milano, holds an MBA from EADA Business School and has a masters in marketing and communication of luxury goods. He has decennial experience in luxury goods, having worked for several companies in the horological industry.

Christophe Sempels holds a doctorate in marketing from the Catholic University of Louvain, Belgium. He is currently Associate Professor of Strategy at SKEMA Business School. He has published extensively about the link between sustainable development, strategy and marketing. He was awarded the Jadde Prize in 2008 for his contribution to the diffusion of sustainable development among companies.

Rasa Stankeviciute is a freelance marketing consultant, specializing in fashion and luxury goods. She holds an MSc degree in international marketing and business development. She is a blogger on her blog *Fashion Population* (http://fashionpopulation.blogspot. com or www.fashionpopulation.com).

___ne Van Gorp recently graduated with an MSc in international marketing and business development from SKEMA Business School. She is currently working as an account manager for the Antwerp-Waasland Chamber of Commerce in Belgium.

INTRODUCTION

Jonas Hoffmann and Ivan Coste-Manière

What exactly do we mean by 'luxury'? Most of us are able to recognize a luxury product, but we are unable to define the specific characteristics that contribute to the concept of luxury. This is because our perception of luxury is individual; it depends on our individual real-life experiences. We each value a different aspect of what we call luxury. It may be to do with rarity, class, quality or comfort. Luxury could be something tailor-made, something special to do, or to own, a privilege, or simply the time to do what we want with our money.

The meaning of luxury and the sorts of customers that buy luxury have continually been evolving, but never as dramatically as in the past 20 years. The sheer number of luxury consumers has exploded as upper- and high class societies are growing around the world. With more potential consumers, the luxury sector is today healthier than ever – increasing at around three times the rate of worldwide wealth.

In the light of these changes, luxury brands have had to completely rethink their strategies and to rely increasingly on state-of-the-art marketing and management tools to help them keep up with consumers' shifting expectations, desires and dreams. There is no place for traditional marketing. Brands that were used to selling high volume to a small, elite group of customers have had to evolve to sell a lower volume to an ever-increasing number of 'ordinary' customers. Brands can no longer rely simply on their name or reputation to maintain market share. Instead, they have to actively compete with other brands on innovation, creativity, distribution, communications and intellectual property. They are forced to build strong brand equities and to balance a far more democratized approach of split markets. The new battlefield is situated in the emerging countries – China, India, Brazil, Russia and Middle East – so a whole new plan of attack is necessary to take into account cultural management and the customers' education.

How should luxury companies be managed in this diverse, global and changing environment? This book aims to answer this question. It provides a myriad of perspectives on what is luxury management nowadays, how it is evolving and which fundamentals are necessary to manage in this time of change. This is done by presenting the view of an international panel of luxury experts. Their common point is that they all are lecturers at SKEMA Business School Master of Science in Luxury and Fashion Management. This book aims to mirror the positioning of this MSc: a multicultural, holistic perspective designed to create challengers to the established rules of the luxury industry.

Ivan Coste-Manière, Katrina Panchout and Jacques Molas present in the chapter 'The Evolution of the Luxury Market: Stairway to Heaven?' the evolution of the luxury industry during the two last decades. They describe a shift from family-owned business to the constitution of large industry conglomerates like LVMH, PPR and Richemont. They then explore the role of Brazil, Russia, India and China in shaping the luxury market of this decade.

Francesco Giliberti Birindelli highlights the complexity of managing a luxury company in the chapter 'Luxury Business: Multinational Organizations and Global Specialization'. He shows how the luxury business can be diversified and complex and gives non-luxury goods practitioners an insight into a typical area of expertise within this sector, as well as the main front- and back-office issues to be analyzed and solved.

Finance plays a central role in business and is paramount as luxury companies go global. Giulio Pizzini discusses in the chapter 'Finance Survival Guide: Value Creation and Piña Coladas' the reason why all businesses exist. He takes a pedagogical approach to explaining in a simple and clear way the basics of financial statements, including balance sheet, income statement, cash flow statement and discounted cash flows.

Jonas and Betina Hoffmann then analyze innovation in the luxury industry. They view innovation as a process comprising four steps: path, insight, excellence in the execution and rareness of experience, symbolized by the acronym PIER. The case of Richard Mille watches exemplifies this process. They conclude by exploring how technology and globalization will shape luxury innovation in the years to come. A clue: emerging countries are the place to be.

Retailing is where it all happens. Alessandro Quintavalle presents a complete review of online and offline luxury retailing design in the chapter 'Retailing in the Luxury Industry'. The store – physical or virtual – represents the most complete experience for real and virtual brand elements and, in order to finalize a sale, all the brand manifestations must be perfectly tuned. Several examples illustrate his proposal.

Fleur Gastaldi then presents the fascinating and complex issue of how luxury brands deal with Internet in the chapter 'Internet, Social Media and Luxury Strategy'. Stakes and costs are high in the luxury industry. The competitive advantage generated by the web would only qualify as successful for the brands that will apprehend the web with brand intelligence, strategic skills and business vision. In the end, what is worth doing offline is also applicable to the online market.

The next two chapters explore branding in the luxury industry. Tinne Van Gorp, in the chapter 'Branding Principles in the Luxury Industry', outlines the main principles needed to build a luxury fashion brand: clear brand identity, marketing communications, product integrity, brand signature, premium prices, exclusivity, heritage, environment and service, and culture. The results of case studies with four luxury leather goods brands are presented.

Rasa Stankeviciute in the chapter 'Brand Extensions in the Luxury Industry' explains that continuous brand extension may result in brand dilution. Companies must find ways to avoid brand extension mistakes and assure that the brand extensions will not dilute the brand with a well-established name for luxury. Four case studies are presented: Rolls-Royce, Mercedes-Benz, Jimmy Choo and Giorgio Armani.

Finally, Christophe Sempels in the chapter 'Sustainable Development in the Luxury Industry: Beyond the Apparent Oxymoron' explains that many drivers should motivate luxury companies to engage in more sustainable business practices. He demonstrates that luxury brands are missing opportunities not to engage in sustainability leadership and provides practical ways to implement sustainable development in luxury companies, at both strategic and operational levels.

As each chapter stands alone, it is not necessary to read the book in any particular order. The authors' varied perspectives provide sound advice on how to manage luxury brands in the years to come, exemplifying luxury strategy in action!

ACKNOWLEDGMENTS

The authors are grateful to the companies and brands that graciously granted us permission to reproduce their company images in this book: Richard Mille, F. lli Pisa Spa and Editions Temps International. We warmly thank Sian Jones for her copy editing. We thank SKEMA Business School for their support. Finally, we thank Stephen Rutt, Eleanor Davey Corrigan, Hannah Fox, Priya Venkat and Palgrave Macmillan.

1

THE EVOLUTION OF THE LUXURY MARKET: STAIRWAY TO HEAVEN?

Ivan Coste-Manière, Katrina Panchout, and Jacques Molas

1.1 INTRODUCTION*

Luxury is the art of fools, said Henri Duvernois.

In the space of 20 years, the luxury market has changed, almost beyond recognition. The narrow range of customer-targeted and the exclusive-distribution channels have been replaced by a stretching of the brand to appeal to and be affordable by a wider range of consumers.

This chapter presents the evolution of the luxury industry from the 1990s through the 2000s and provides a perspective for the 2010s with the rise of luxury consumption in markets such as Brazil, Russia, China and India or the United Arab Emirates. It concludes by giving advice on how to manage in the years to come.

1.2 THE LUXURY INDUSTRY 1990–2000: STARTING THE CHANGE

Over one century, the French fashion sector changed gradually from a home-made world with a large knowledge to an activity of mass production addressing a wider market. But it is in the beginning of the 1990s that the luxury industry has been redefined and reoriented. Designers and fashion designers became art directors. According to Jollant-Kneebone and Bernstein,[1] at the end of the 80s, luxury was a world where we were between ourselves, a house, not a company. These houses had regular customers. The world of luxury was a closed and very elitist universe, but one which changed with the arrival of large luxury groups such as PPR, Prada or LVMH. Then since the 90s, the luxury industry underwent a revolution with the arrival of marketing. Luxury differs and has to adapt itself to the evolution of the market and of the society to affect everybody.

The French Economic and Social Council[2] reminded us in 2008 that at the beginning of the 1970s most luxury companies were in fact 'shops' making a turnover of some million francs. By the middle of the 1990s, the situation was quite different. How, in the space of ten years, did the luxury sector change into a real industry, with large groups and an industrial logic based on diversification and internationalization? The answer is the stock exchange.

1.2.1 The creation of large groups

The Economic and Social Council examined the new economic logics that dominated the luxury sector: 1) the passage of a home-made logic into an industrial logic – companies managed to launch this logic by developing production while preserving the quality of the work and the product; 2) the managerial mimicry, financial logic that showed itself as an essential element of the new strategies; and 3) the creation of international luxury groups, allowing the promotion of an increasing number of brands on the markets, was one of the distinctive facts of the 1990s.

The context was not very good in the 1990s, but many people believed that luxury was synonymous with continuous growth with record dividends. From Alain Chevalier to Louis Racamier, many entrepreneurs invested in this sector to create new groups, but were forced to give up as they were unable to assume the development costs. However, while failure is not a surprise, the fall of Alain Chevalier, who had hoisted Moët-Hennessy to the highest level of the wines and spirit houses in the 1970s, was unexpected. Ousted from the Louis Vuitton-Moët-Hennessy group in 1989 (after successfully overseeing the fusion in 1987), Chevalier tried to create a new luxury company by taking back (at a very high price – 500 million francs) the Balmain Company. Less than one year later, he gave up fashion design. The profitability was not there.

Louis Racamier, who put Louis Vuitton at the top of the travel goods table, experienced a similar story. Racamier was also at the origin of the fusion of the family group Racamier with Moët-Hennessy, creating the first world luxury group. He also initiated the entrance of Bernard Arnault into the company only to be ousted by him later. As a form of revenge, Louis Racamier established a new group, Orcofi. Supported by his whole family – the Vuitton heirs – as well as by L'Oreal, he bought the respectable house of Lanvin (for 500 million francs), at the beginning of the 1990s, with the objective of restoring its lost prestige, and the luxury caterer Hédiard. He also financed the creation of a subsidiary with the name of Inès de la Fressange, a former Chanel model. However, the luxury crisis of 1993, a consequence of the first Gulf War, a risky management and huge expenses reduced all his projects, and in 1994 he had to give up Lanvin to L'Oreal and sell its other shares to Axa in 1996, with the exception of the leather worker Andrelux, which was placed in receivership in 1997.

Bernard Arnault, on the other hand, having successfully created the big group, LVMH in 1989, is still present in numerous luxury sectors, fashion and perfume, from Château d'Yquem to Moët & Chandon. At the end of the 1990s, François Pinault tried a similar operation and became the main French competitor of LVMH, with a turnover of 1.5 billion francs. Hermes, well managed by Jean-Louis Dumas, also managed to constitute a group and to diversify its productions. Creating a new brand image, Hermes was relatively successful in table art with the purchase of the crystal glass manufacturer of Saint Louis and the silversmith Puiforcat. Abroad, the group Vendôme, the property of the Richemont family, is the main competitor of the French brands, holding an impressive portfolio of brands such as Cartier or Baume & Mercier, or Van Cleef & Arpels.

The perfume sector also underwent a period of transformation during the 1990s. LVMH with the support of Dior, L'Oreal, Procter & Gamble, Unilever and Wella controls all the industry. The world of the perfume tended to become a manufacturer of cosmetics, much closer to the chemical industry than to the luxury sector. In fact, in the 1990s, Elf was one of the first companies of the perfume market through its subsidiary Sanofi that owned in particular Saint Laurent perfume before giving up these brands to Gucci.

Thus, the 1990s were characterized by the creation of large groups and a shift from a home-made logic to an industrial logic.

1.2.2 The shift from a home-made logic to an industrial logic

As in all heavy industries, the luxury industry tried to define strategies of integration. Thus, the group LVMH had three big poles. The 'wines and spirit' activity was organized around the brands of Champagne (Moët & Chandon, Haberdasher, De Venoge, Veuve Clicquot, and so on), Cognacs and Spirits, and also around the production of the foreign, American and Chilean domains. A second pole constituted luggage and leather with the brands of Berluti, Céline, Loewe and Vuitton. The third was fashion and perfumes with Givenchy, Kenzo, Lacroix (sold in 2006), Dior or Guerlain. This activity was prolonged by the control of retail chains – Sephora acquired in 1997 and Marie-Jeanne Godard in 1999 – and duty-free shops (DFS) for duty-free sales.

These industrialists no longer adopted an approach directly linked to luxury, but followed instead a commercial and industrial logic. Marketing became the dominant notion with the concept of large-scale production. The example of perfumes in the LVMH group confirms this new orientation. LVMH, the giant of the perfume industry, produced all the various ranges of fragrances, from the prestigious brands of Dior or Kenzo to low-priced perfumes, in the same laboratories and the same factories. Thus, during the 1990s, the luxury industry underwent a process of industrial standardization, and the luxury product became a product like any other. If we take the example of perfume, nowadays, the non-specialized perfumes have to seduce everybody, the Americans as well as the Japanese. The high quality standards are being lost and perfume has become a convenience good. The explosion in the number of perfumes launched in the market and the shortening of the life cycle of each of them correspond to the same logic as other products of other industries.

This evolution has also affected Haute Couture. Haute Couture has progressively disappeared, replaced with a form of ready-to-wear clothing, renamed 'top of the range' to justify its high prices. In practically ten years, the number of Parisian fashion houses has been halved: 24 in 1987, down to 12 in 1997. This figure fell to ten at the end of 2005. Balmain, Chanel, Dior, Gaultier, Givenchy, Hanae Mori, Lacroix, Scherrer, Torrente Ungaro, all closed their workshops from 2003 to 2005.

The arts of fashion and perfume henceforth entered the industry of mass consumption.

1.2.3   The importance of marketing and the concept of diversification

During the 1990s we witnessed, along with the new profit-seeking financial logic, a diversification of the brand and the lending of the label to any type of product, sometimes without much discernment. It became important, as the marketing discourse of the moment stated, to make customers a global offer comprising many products. These product variations could be positioned 'horizontally' (as seen in extensions of Gucci's ready-to-wear and watches, Louis Vuitton dresses, Boucheron in perfumes, and so on) or 'vertically' (more complex to manage), with additional positions (variations of brands and sub-brands Max Mara, or, to a lesser degree, of Escada and Armani with new segments: Semi Deluxe evening, sports, young, strong women). These variations need to be created under the control of marketing and depend for their success on the control of distribution.

For example, during this period all the product managers and communication directors dreamed of producing pens and watches. Thus, jewelers, perfumers and fashion designers began to offer watch collections for men and women. The only commercial success, however, came from Chanel. At the same time, all brands wanted to sell their own perfume. Again, not always successfully – Bucheron being a notable exception – as development costs were so high that the company often had to sacrifice its independence (Lalique, for example). Today, more than 200 top brand perfumes are launched every year.

This trend of diversification has brought with it a new practice in the luxury industry, that of outsourcing. When a brand branches out into a new product range, it obviously does not have the necessary skills and equipment in-house. Neither Roche nor Hermes has the equipment to make table products, nor can Christofle produce clothes or crystal. At the beginning, cooperation is established between the different brands. In 1990, porcelain, sold under the name Christofle, was produced by large companies in Limoges. The Hermes jewelry was made by Christofle. Gradually, however, the brand started looking to reduce its costs. Porcelain could be sourced more cheaply not in Limoges, but in Portugal or Tunisia. The jewelry is manufactured in Thailand and the crystals in Arques (Pas-de-Calais).

This period also saw the creation of a brand that is attached to a particular product. One example might be the creation of the brand and its perfume Paloma Picasso. Here, the origins of the brand are forgotten and new associations are created. The silverware brand Christofle, which is diversifying into jewelry and watches, is a good example. In haute couture, however, the result may be disastrous, as was the case with the concepts of Porno Chic, Look Trash and Glam-Trash with Dior and its creator, John Galliano.

1.2.4 New markets, new opportunities: The internationalization of the luxury industry

After industrialization and diversification, the final major transformation in the luxury industry during the 1990s was internationalization. On one hand, there was a huge potential of growth in the emerging countries. The big brands had enough weight to support a country risk and take advantage of this growth, but, on the other hand, it was necessary to pay off, on a wide base, the investments of the collection and the development of the concepts (products and distribution). Brands that limited themselves to the national market were thus confronted with problems not only of growth but also of profitability. Nowadays, the necessary investments to develop and manage concepts that can create some value in the luxury are no longer enough to compete only in one country.

Over these ten years, the place of the luxury industry in international trade has become increasingly important, showing the recognition of the quality of the sold products. In 1993, the companies of the Colbert committee made a turnover from exports in excess of 20 billion francs (3.2 billion euros). Of the total turnover, 73 percent was made in the international trade. Another professional source, including the French confederacy of the art professions, gave a turnover of 39 billion francs for export (6 billion euros) – 44 percent of the total figure of business. Most of the French exports were directed toward three destinations: Western Europe, North America, and Japan. Even if China did not appear in the statistics, it already seemed to have a strong outlet potential and to be a big competitor for the future. This growth was largely related to the arrival of a new kind of customer and the density of tourists, especially Asian customers. Due to the high price of luxury goods in Asia (about 30 percent higher than in Western countries because of tariffs, barriers or Supply Chain Management), especially in Japan, Asian consumers became important customers of luxury off-Asia.

The emergence of a new customer with high purchasing power is also a determining factor of the growth of this sector in the international trade. It helps boost sales. Thus, the 1990s and the arrival of new markets gave the luxury industry incredible new opportunities of development and success.

1.3 THE LUXURY INDUSTRY 2000–2010: GLOBAL LUXURY ACTIVITIES

The success of the luxury market during the twentieth century was due in part to the creation of a new social class, the bourgeoisie. Well-known designers, such as Coco Chanel, Christian Dior or Jeanne Lanvin, made their name at this time when the concept of luxury was clearly defined in the minds of the consumer.

Today, the definition of luxury has lost some of this clarity. How can we define something that is present at so many levels and in such a diverse range of products? Pure luxury no longer exists. The whole concept of luxury is changing, both anticipating and following the constant shift of consumers' dreams, needs and desires. However, it is important for luxury to stay at the forefront of this evolution – a highly protected 'avant garde': consistent, superior, innovative, design quality and services are concepts which have been repeated so many times, they do not mean anything more within the 'mass market' word but for particular opportunities.

Being aware of customer needs and being more competitive means that companies must change while maintaining their core values, extending their ranges, refreshing, stretching and offering more affordable products for the so-called upper market. Luxury brands have expanded with new names and with new horizons. Different categories of brands have been introduced such as 'premium brands', 'niche brands', 'creators brands', 'top of the range brands', 'luxury sewing'. The brands have to face a problem of identity and positioning. The new technologies and communication that have been developed over these last years have contributed to the democratization of luxury.

Are you an elitist or a democrat? For the former, luxury is reserved for a small educated minority. For the latter, access to luxury should be as broad as possible. Historically elitist, the luxury goods sector has tended, over the past 15 years, to embrace democracy. An increasing number of occasional customers, as opposed to the traditional customer-exclusive, come to shop, claiming a 'right of luxury'. These customers are greater in number, but they buy less. Of course, luxury is luxury and there is no question that it loses its image quality or rarity. By this, we mean that an increasing number of people can afford a couple of designer pieces without becoming regular customers, often because they can simply not afford.

There are no real barriers anymore in the consumption of luxury items, and we see new trends appearing which associate clothes from Zara or H&M with others from Prada, Dior or Gucci. The clientele of the luxury today is very heterogeneous.

This democratization is classified by Silverstein and Fiske (2003) on the basis of three types of goods[3]:

- Accessible superpremium: Products which are the most expensive ones in their category but affordable by middle market consumers; these are 'low ticket items'.
- Old-luxury brand extensions: These are brands that are 'lower-priced version of goods that have traditionally been affordable only by the rich'. This means that brands extended their range to attract more people.

■ Mass prestige or 'Masstige': It is 'far from being the highest-priced product in a category'. This is a mix between mass and class; less expensive than superpremium goods. This allows everybody to have access to luxury goods and all brands, to reach a maximum number of consumers who are generally nicknamed the 'luxury tourists'.

In fact, the new concept of luxury is a recent phenomenon – only some ten years old, as depicted by the LV and Burberry cases[4] – and one that is more accessible, in contrast with the old luxury which used to be a heritage brand, and affirms that 'heritage and prestige are the hallmarks of many luxury brands, some of which are hundreds of years old. The enduring quality of a particular luxury good can be part of its appeal, yet consumers – particularly young, fashion-conscious consumers – want a product that looks fresh and unexpected.'

The fact that luxury brands have moved into emerging countries has also contributed to the diversification of the luxury customer profile. The customer has become more casual and particularly more diverse in terms of culture.

Do luxury brands prefer to sell to elites or to diversify/expand their customer base? It really depends on the market vision adopted by each luxury business manager. Some prefer to stick to a core group of preferred customers and regulars. They tend not to adopt their trade policies according to the target or country. Others, who have followed the evolution of the luxury market, have decided to make their offer more accessible by offering cheaper products for, in particular, a younger audience.

1.3.1 Luxury according to incomes, ages or genders

Surveys on luxury consumers such as the Unity Marketing Luxury Tracking Report, or by Merrill Lynch, have shown a fairly even and obviously Gaussian distribution for all income levels. There are more and more consumers attracted by the now famous 'hyper luxury' (business jets with Dassault and Grumman as world leaders and Embraer on the edge, space shuttles with more and more competitors among others). These new categories and consumer segments follow an entropic growth which is much better analyzed by the famous power's law, with a longer and longer tail. Unity Marketing's exclusive Luxury Consumption Index, among many others, can be used as a wonderful barometer to check out the market's evolution.

The baby boomer generation represents a great potential, but the now famous GenXers seem to be as money conscious as the GenYers who might be considered as a great opportunity for marketers. It is difficult to give a concise definition of these two conceptual segments as they used to be age based and they are now much more led by behavioral analysis. This is also to be applied to the border between fashion and luxury, if we could admit luxury to become fashion, and tailor-made offers to become mimetic.

Linked to the evolution which has been noticed from 1995, the empowered women, *konagus* in Japan, have been establishing an average 65/35 percent (female- vs male-driven consumption) ratio. The U point was reached in 2005. It seems as if a female-driven market such as the one once emphasized by the series *Sex and the City*, and which has long ago been studied for the diamond industry, has been reducing the males' purchases.

To sum up, the luxury perception of consumers is no longer what it used to be. People's needs and expectations have changed. Today they buy luxury products and services for different reasons, such as, to impress others, self-direct pleasure, self-gift giving, and of course for quality.

This drives companies to adapt their marketing communication strategies, by using an Integrated Marketing Communication (IMC). In fact, luxury brands use tools such as advertising, public relations and sponsorship. In addition, companies are widening their range, in order to reach more consumers, by creating new market segments and are adapting their advertising to each target.

The abrupt change in terms of consumer behavior modifications is making companies adapt their marketing strategies, influencing driving and being driven by the market, improving and increasing the scope of the most sophisticated, integrated communication strategies.

What do the 2010s hold? A shift to luxury in emerging countries is the most certain answer.

1.4 THE 2010s: EMERGING COUNTRIES TAKE THE LEAD

As expected by many analyses, in 2007 the worldwide wealth increased by 9.4 percent reaching 41 trillion dollars. Even though the USA was still ranked first, the top list of the richest countries has definitely changed. The evolution of GDP in developing countries could even be increasing during this period with astonishing facts and figures. There are numerous countries, depicting young and numerous populations, within which the wealth coud be increasing at a rate of 20 percent. India, in 2007, showed one of the best growth rates – an incredible 22.7 percent, China 20.3 percent and Brazil 19.1 percent. During these years, at LVMH and others, the common strategic analysis was to consider a third of the luxury products as being sold to Brazil, India, and China, followed by Russia within the next ten years, making these citizens the largest luxury consumers by 2015.

In the next decade, the joint revenues of these markets will surpass those of most of the traditional established markets in Europe, North America, and Japan. They will drive the continuous evolution of luxury. Chanel has understood this evolution with some Chinese collections, the occidental luxury culture imposition gradually giving way to the oriental luxury consumption style, and to the mall culture, an approach that is much more devoted to these new consumers and to this multi-ethno-driven potential market. A wonderful and strategic ten-year-long bet. The global distribution chain is changing from flagships to retailing point of sales. As Uché Okonkwo explained,

> brands such as Burberry currently have more Russian clients in several UK locations than residents, and these new clients will continue to perceive luxury through different sets of references and parameters. These market dynamics are changing the luxury landscape, and therefore luxury management practices require revisiting and refining to accommodate these paradoxes.[5]

1.4.1 Brazil

Brazil, where there were more than 140,000 US$ millionaires in 2007, increased the consumption of global luxury products by

17 percent that year. Brazil lacks a real luxury culture, and Brazil's luxury consumers are among the most discerning. It is a resilient, dynamic, energetic and impulsive country, with a high future-oriented culture of appearance and image. Brazilians, like many young populations around the globe, are crazy about pleasure and entertainment; it is the hedonic market of today. When dealing with products, Brazilians expect exclusive limited edition products, the old Spanish way around 2000. This high selectivity impacts on distribution so that this highly selective distribution could be 'felt' in very exclusive locations.

Mexico, with Carlo Corinto, used the same battle plan around 2000. Refined communications media, changing the intrinsic essence of the message, with direct and effective reaches and targeted brand with private sales must therefore be used. This exclusivity perception makes counterfeits accepted when bought by tourists but not by locals.

As expected by analysts such as AT Kearney's team, Brazil still needs some retail network expansion, and, above all, consumer knowledge and 'central' consumer groups need to be improved.

1.4.2 Russia

The Russian luxury market today reaches 7 percent of the world-wide market. It is expected to grow about 30 percent on average. The fall of the iron curtain led Russian millionaires and *nouveaux riches* to spend even without thinking. There too, Russian wealthy people have been starting to seek knowledge and experiences. Russia, a rich, strong, passionate and spirited, driven and daring country, is fond of glamour, very past, present and future oriented, improving its knowledge-conscious orientation – thus making it a very challenging market. Russian luxury consumers and retail distribution channels exist for today. As frequent buyers, Russian citizens expect products to show a balance between heritage, tradi-tion, modesty and wealth. The bling-bling orientation is definitely not the one and only trend. Distribution should focus on limited access, private, exclusive shopping, with a much wider range of products than anywhere else except maybe in the Emirates. Being very respectful when talking about the roots and territories of their best-loved brands, the Russian fans expect a huge brand heritage and have very vast product knowledge. Counterfeits are much more tracked than before. As most of the return on investment in this country seems to be almost achieved for many companies, a change in the consumer attitudes and behaviors is expected, with an increase in the luxury services to consumer related to the growth of wealth in Russia.

1.4.3 China

China is today considered as a miracle in a country where the luxury consumer market was almost nonexistent some 20 years ago. Nowadays, this market is predicted to be almost unstoppable. The growth of the Chinese GDP has led almost all luxury groups to invest heavily in China. This blitzkrieg which started in this region from Hong Kong, between 2005 and 2010, targeted the Chinese tourists first, as they could still be considered as elite; the number of passengers grew at a yearly rate of 10 percent. China is heavily dynamic, present and long-term oriented, very much social-status conscious, progressive, promising. Despite economic progress, China remains volatile. The Chinese luxury consumer is already there today while Chinese luxury retail might be for tomorrow, except for malls. Chinese expect an outwardly visible luxury, status-driven products, going shopping with friends. Stores and prices are to be designed so that they are more accessible, a wider portfolio of products being vital. The brand awareness is to be designed locally for cross-channel purchases. A huge problem in China is that this country is currently listed as one of the major con-tributors to the counterfeit luxury industry, increasing drastically unexpected cannibalization. China is mature enough, whatever the risks are, for future tremendous market growth with more and more educated sophisticated clients and much more customization and personalization as the individualism level will increase, thanks to grown-up 'little emperors'.

1.4.4 India

India is the biggest democracy in the world with almost 50 percent of its population under 20 years old. Predicted to be the fifth luxury market by 2025, the trend is more than optimistic as the consumption is estimated to increase by four. Many have forgotten that luxury companies were able to survive around 1929, thanks to maharajahs. This country has the best knowledge, and most of the best goodwill and know-how. More than 125,000 US$ millionaires currently exist. But, most Indians being money conscious have a slightly lower appetite for luxury. India is currently seeking how to spend its wealth, the reflective and/or the mentalizing way. The Indian luxury consumer is for tomorrow, the Indian luxury is for today. From reflective brands such as TAG Heuer with the living God SRK, to the most mentalizing heritage hotels (Neemrana Hotels of our friends Aman Nath and Francis Wacziarg 'no hotel hotels'); it is easy to feel how energetic, knowledgeable, young, and dynamic India is. The culture of style, of haute couture with designers such as Malini Ramni, or HiDesign created in 1978 by Dilip Kapur, balances present and future orientations in the meantime.

Like China, success is the definitive hunt. Being the kings of hospitality and service, stylish Indian customers expect beautiful products and luxury complimentary additional services. The atmosphere of the points of sales is crucial in luxury boutiques which are, for most part, located in luxury malls (such as DLF Emporio in Delhi, Gold Souk in Cochin), with a browsing experience. Very respectful, the Indian customers need real curate brand knowledge and an Indian celebrity endorsement. Counterfeits are generally ignored, but this attitude is unfortunately changing. The new India appeared in 1992 and a careful retail infrastructure development must be led, much more adapted to mass luxury, and dissimilar poly-ethnic or incomes-centered consumer segments.

Heritage Hotels as Luxury by Ravi Shanker[6]

The Heritage Hotels in India have mushroomed due to several reasons. A rich architectural and cultural heritage lies preserved in them. The concept started from the royal state of Rajasthan where the present royal families could not maintain their huge properties without assistance. The mansions were converted into hotels to offer travellers to the land a unique and unforgettable experience. The Heritage Hotels thus born were followed elsewhere in the country too. Many of them required years of restoration, reconstruction, and renovation to make them suitable for international tourists.

Established hotel players like Taj and Oberoi showcase their heritage properties with pride. Taj manages palaces and rustic safari lodges like Fort Aguada Beach Resort in Goa, Usha Kiran Palace in Gwalior, Rambagh Palace in Jaipur, Umaid Bhawan Palace in Jodhpur, and Sawai Madhopur Lodge at Ranthambore in Sawai Madhopur. Oberoi have heritage properties like Oberoi Cecil in Shimla, and Maidens in Delhi.

Many major hoteliers are acquiring the old forts and havelis and converting them into luxurious hotels and resorts. The best example is that of ITC group who is playing a significant role in developing heritage into luxury business. WelcomHeritage, one of the chains of hotels in the ITC group, brings together a chain of palaces, forts, havelis, and resorts that offer a unique experience. WelcomHeritage endeavors to preserve ancient royal homes and the historical Indian grandeur and opulence for future Indian generations.

The Neemrana Group of Hotels, another player in the hospitality industry has not so much raised the bar of Indian hospitality, but has worked concertedly towards creating another niche whereby the experiencing of history and its architectural treasures has now become a part of the Indian tourism repertoire. It is for this 'experiential authenticity' that the Neemrana 'non-hotel' Hotels have now come to be known.[7]

Rajasthan, the land of kings, is the largest state of India. It is one of the most sought after states in the country in terms of tourism and holidays in India. It attracts tourists through out the entire globe with its rich culture & tradition, heritage, and glorious past.

The above-mentioned countries should allow the growth of the world wealth estimated at around 60 trillion dollars by the year 2012 with an average increase of 7.7 percent compared to 2007. Growth rates such as 10 percent for Africa, 8 percent for Pacific Asia, 11 percent for Latin America and even 15 percent for the Middle East are expected, an entropic growth which is nowhere else recorded. Even in 'stagnant' economies figures are interesting; the North America and Europe luxury markets are to increase at a lower speed of 6.8 percent and 4.9 percent, which is far above the growth of the GDPs and wealth.

1.5 FROM HERE TO ETERNITY

We have seen over the past 20 years that the concept of luxury has evolved radically. As incomes have risen, so has the demand for luxury, and this increased demand, from a far wider range of consumers, means that luxury has become more difficult to define. As it is no longer limited to an elite class, the price-quality dimension is not a sufficient criterion. Today's luxury consumers are less concerned than in the past with social status and prestige, and with the intrinsic ownership of the luxury item. They are more concerned by the whole luxury experience: an experience that includes innovative design, consistent quality, and superior service over time.

To keep pace with such radical changes in the concept of luxury, luxury brands have to be more competitive, innovative and aware of customers' slightest needs, dreams and desires. Brand stretching, as personal incomes rose, made luxury marketers able to offer less luxurious product lines at more reasonable prices. This typical avalanche diffusion model boosts the audiences, and slightly reduces the affinities.

Market surveys are declining as they are already off as soon as released, giving place to pure trend-spotting analysis. Having flair is of major importance when talking about strategies or launches. These abrupt changes came from great consumer behavior modifications, which have been leading companies to adapt their marketing strategies. It is commonly admitted that all the different crisis from 1992 to nowadays (from Gulf wars to SARS, or financial crisis, or 9/11 attacks) have been favoring a price-hunter feeling among consumers.

The confrontation to the explosion of unexpected distribution channels (parallel importation, gray market, vintage, second-hand) has been making luxury brands react by at least influencing better the market and improving their communication strategy, using more and more endorsement and celebrities and refreshing René Girard's mimetic theory. In the meantime, the consolidation of the listed luxury and fashion companies has also been following the same trend, while most of them could keep on protecting and increasing their 'brand value' and brand- and consumers-based equities.

Finally, the frontal confrontation between different generations is occurring more than anywhere else in the luxury world. Each generation has precise and different relationships with luxury. What used to be age concerned is now increasingly being driven by behaviors. These greater and greater differentiations are driven by the background evolution of social, political, and economic factors. In terms of social neighborhood pressures, each generation is influenced by the preceding generation's relationship to luxury. In other words, and for once, we could be talking about a 'cultural mimicry' which is to be almost opposed to 'communication and advertising'. From modernists to postmodernists and followers, the shift has been almost perpetual. The greatest coincidence comes from the fact that the lean, Generation-X 'less is more' philosophy of the 1990s has been preceded and then immediately followed by the baby boomer's conspicuous consumption ideals of the 1980s.

Luxury used to be a mink fur coat, a Cadillac car, sticking to the 3Rs (Rolex, Rolls Royce, Riviera) complex. Today, the greatest luxury might be time. A full and complete revival of hedonism can be expected, as the one observed within the cosmetic industry with the so-called spa effect.

It is definitely time to live and enjoy life, to stick to more and more refined lifestyles, keeping us healthy and balanced. In other words, luxury can still be regarded as a stairway to heaven, but a stairway that is accessible to all, whatever their spending power.

ACKNOWLEDGMENTS

I dedicate this chapter to the memory of my mentors Edmond Roudnitska Paul Teisseire and Pierre Soustelle who created L'Air du Temps, Han Paul Bodifee Chairman of Prodarom. The sections 'The luxury industry 1990–2000: Starting the change' and 'The luxury industry 2000–2010: Global luxury activities' are adapted from a report by SKEMA MSc students Lucile Egal, Martin Favre-Felix, and Alexandre Lanoue whom I thank for their work. Finally, I warmly thank Ruchita Sharma, Aman Nath, Jean Claude Novaro, and Richard Mille, and all my friends and artists at Dassault, RSW AF Corse, MPM Monaco.

2

LUXURY BUSINESS: MULTINATIONAL ORGANIZATIONS AND GLOBAL SPECIALIZATIONS

Francesco Giliberti Birindelli

2.1 INTRODUCTION TO THE ORGANIZATIONAL COMPLEXITY OF THE LUXURY BUSINESS

The purpose of this chapter is to show how diversified and complex the luxury business is and to give non-luxury goods practitioners an insight into the typical areas of expertise within this sector, and the main front and back-office issues to analyze and solve.

The luxury business is, by far, one of the most complex and wide-ranging businesses present in the market.

A luxury brand is a global competitor that has to face not only all the global issues but the local issues as well.

For the success of the brand, decision makers in the luxury business have to manage a number of core issues on a daily basis. These include creativity, marketing, production, quality control and monitoring, sourcing of raw materials, market penetration, merchandizing, the retail and wholesale distribution chain, and store planning. In addition to these issues, they also face a controversial and crucial trade-off: market expansion against organizational complexity of administration, compliance, tax and customs, among others.

The luxury business as a whole represents a surprisingly thin niche market, formed by, and includes several sub-niches that can easily be streamlined in the main sub-sectors. These are fashion, wines and spirits, watches, accessories, perfumes and fragrances.

Although rather difficult to understand intuitively, or at a first glance, the luxury business as a whole (including the above-referenced sectors) weighs less than, or the same as, some of the world's largest companies taken individually. For example, in terms of gross income, companies such as General Electric, Walmart, Royal Dutch Shell, Exxon Mobil, BP and Toyota show turnovers ranging from $400 to $200 billion. The luxury goods market taken as a whole, on the other hand, has a turnover in the range of $260–$280 billion.[1]

This helps to put the luxury sector into perspective and highlights the difficulty facing luxury businesses of competing in a global market with very limited resources in terms of human, economic and administrative back-office.

2.2 A BUSINESS MADE UP EXCLUSIVELY OF HUMAN EXPERTISE

Craftsmanship is the key factor that differentiates fashion from luxury. These two concepts are often confused. In contrast with fashion, luxury, which is made up primarily of craftsmanship, icon, prestige and symbol, cannot be industrialized easily, and rarely benefits from economies of scale. Nor can it be exported to low-cost countries to reduce the cost side of the group's profits and losses.

Consider the following example: Imagine you have €100,000 to 'invest' in what could be described as man's favorite gadget – a luxury wristwatch.

Simply by walking into the store you can have, in 5 minutes, the stunning and outstandingly complicated, automatic, world-wide time control (also known as the *ore del mondo* watch), gold wrist watch with a crocodile bracelet and ruby and emerald mountings.

Have you ever thought about what lies behind the €100,000 you may have paid to buy this...gadget?

Raw materials (main supplies required):

– Gold – this precious metal comes from South Africa. It is traded on stocks markets and commonly sold in US dollars. It will be imported, and duties will be paid at the time of the import, before being manufactured.

- Precious stones – rubies, coming from India, East Africa or South America, and emeralds, coming primarily from Russia, Colombia, probably purchased and traded in the Antwerp Market of Precious Stones. Circulation is strictly regulated.
- Crocodile bracelet – this may be seen as the simplest of the components, but...where does the crocodile skin come from? It can be from Egypt or the United States (primarily Missouri and Louisiana), and the trade of these precious skins is strictly regulated by the Washington Convention (more about this later).

By the time all the raw materials have been collected, the manufacturer has made a considerable effort and capital investment (without yet considering the design, sampling, prototyping and engineering of the product!), but the desired wristwatch still has a long way to go before reaching the shop! The next phase concerns manufacturing and craftsmanship:

- The bracelet – of course tanning and manufacturing the precious crocodile skin is not the watchmaker's business. It is a specific and complex activity performed by a few craftsman mostly located in certain regions of Italy and France.
- The stones – cutting a stone requires skill and experience and very few specialists around the world know how to do it. This is a globe-trotting business – diamonds are cut in India, emeralds in...
- The watch, case and mechanisms – a complicated watch cannot be manufactured in low-labor-cost countries or industrialized in a dedicated plant! Of the high-end watch industries, 80 percent come from Switzerland, from the La Chaux de Fond area where almost all the skills of each single craftsman are employed in the manufacture of each single spare part of the watch.

After having spent a huge amount of time and resources (not to mention the headaches) it is now time to assemble the watch and to ship it to the store where it will be sold.

The simplified example above illustrates why most actors in the luxury business share the same characteristics. Their companies are[2]:

– small (up to €100 million gross income) and medium (from €100 to €500 million gross income);
– family owned;
– have their administrative and production sites in high-cost countries (mainly France and Italy – and Switzerland for watches – counting up to 80 percent of the total revenues of the sector worldwide);
– employ limited human resources, from some hundreds to a few thousand employees.

All these elements define the craftsmanship, entrepreneurship, vision and taste of the owner, who is often also the founder, who has the necessity and opportunity to keep the entire chain under control, from production to retail distribution.

On the other hand, in the world of globalization, the appetite of luxury customers from the four continents is growing and luxury goods players must, if they wish to survive, follow the trends and the customers in their respective home countries.

This is why luxury brand managers must be diligent and, to some extent, brave!

2.3 BOOSTING SPECIALIZED NICHES

As said, managing luxury means managing complex, specialized areas of craftsmanship coupled with managing the consequent administrative and compliance burden.

As an example, the typical group of luxury ready-to-wear companies will encompass at least six different types of companies/divisions specializing in each phase of the business, from the bottom to the top. These phases are:

1. Trademark and creation;
2. Sampling and prototyping;
3. Sourcing, industrialization and manufacturing;

4. Pricing;
5. Wholesale distribution, commercial, customer care and logistics;
6. Retail distribution.

1. Trademark and creation

What pays for a trademark? Who pays the trademark owner for using its logo, insigne, notoriety and global awareness? How are these immaterial rights remunerated?

The answer is royalties!

Many entrepreneurs are happy to pay royalties to well-established brands in order to open monobrand stores, manufacture and distribute wholesale goods, commercialize fragrances and gadgets and so on.

All these entrepreneurs consider the fact that exploiting a well-known brand will allow them to generate good revenues and give up a portion of their profits to remunerate the trademark owner with a royalty based on sales or similar rules.

The trade-off given by the trademark is the so-called luxury-emotion that lies in the binomial heritage-creation, and, as all in luxury, managing the two is complex and time consuming.

Managing creation is tricky. Creators are stars, emotionally explosive and impossible to coach. Have you ever tried limiting creativity? Imposing budgets to samples, or short-listing the sourcing of raw materials for economic purposes? ... not easy, or more accurately, nearly impossible!

As is summarized below, managing a brand is an act of faith involving incertitude and risk. Managing the administrative and back-office side of this work is therefore complex as it deals with the reality of luxury and fashion: managing counterparties all over the world, licensing and protecting rights related to the trademark, fighting against counterfeiting, managing taxes in each country of activity and so on.

2. Sampling and prototyping

Sampling and prototyping are, to some extent, the most crucial and expensive part of the luxury business.

Creating a collection is meaningless if it is not developed into samples to enliven the catwalk, and afterwards into industrialized prototypes for production.

Prototyping will include deciding whether to continue into production, as it will map out the industrialization that is required to manufacture goods destined for sale to the public.

3. Sourcing and manufacturing

Once the product has moved from the catwalk to the prototyping laboratory, the sourcing of raw materials takes place, and it includes several economic, stylistic, creative, administrative and logistic concerns.

In sourcing the raw materials, of course, it is necessary to consider the mixture of stylistic and creative needs of the head of design, the merchandizing, as well as purely economic concerns in order to guarantee the correct industrial cost of the goods to be produced and sold.

Finally, the raw materials may need specific back-office treatment in terms of authorizations, quotas, duties and custom clearance (a detailed list of CITES products can be found in the Appendix).

4. Pricing

The pricing manager has to take into account and mix several key elements that will drive the success of the product. These include:

– The price of similar products proposed to the potential customers by competitors (this is also part of merchandizing and marketing intelligence).
– The industrial cost of the goods, allowing decent gross margins on each product both on the wholesale and on the retail level.
– Currency exchange rates and fluctuations.
– Customs on imports.

Consideration of these elements drives the suggested retail price for each country in which the merchandize is sold. This suggested price list is then circulated to retailers.

The retail price list includes premiums or discounts and takes into account the regional success of the brand as a single element and of the luxury market as a whole.

Pricing lists made by a European luxury *Maison* would normally look like this (Table 2.1):

TABLE 2.1 **Retail suggested price list (including local sale taxes, if any)**

Europe	UK*	USA	Japan	Taiwan	Hong Kong	China	Other Asia
100	103	105	130	115	110	107	105

*In local currency fixed at the 1st of January of each year.

5. Wholesale distribution, commercial, customer care and logistics

The wholesale side of the business manages several clients' accounts, independent stores, shop-in-shop, corners, monobrand or multibrand, related or unrelated, around the world.

While taking orders, following shipment windows and terms of deliveries (called Incoterms[3]) and payment conditions, relationship managers and customer care personnel must understand the culture of their clients and deal with relatively sophisticated international trade concerns, in terms of legal agreements with counterparties, liabilities, freight-forwarding of merchandize and so on.

6. Retail distribution

The final part of the entire value chain ends in the retail distribution, which can be managed using different strategies.

Main competitors of the luxury field, mainly in ready-to-wear and leather goods and accessories such as Louis Vuitton, Gucci, Hermès, would tend to have direct control over this channel, which is the outmost of their access point to the market (from 70 to 100 percent of the source of incomes from the outside world).

By controlling the retail channel, they have full control of the retail environment (physical impact of the store), the control of prices to retail customers. (A few high-end brands, such as Louis Vuitton and Hermès, never mark down their products).

Other competitors, with lower financial resources or different commercial strategies, will balance direct retail penetration with wholesale or licensing, allowing increasing margins and cash flow.

It is easy to understand that direct distribution via directly operated stores triggers a relevant investment in terms of capital expenditure, and may, in some circumstance, dilute margins of the company. On the other hand, as seen, the control of the retail distribution enhances the trademark positioning and valorization.

2.4 HOW TO SPOT THE COMPLEXITY

The profile of a group of medium-sized luxury goods companies, with a good balance of retail and wholesale activity, could be described like this:

- Turnover of 300 million
- Total number of employees 500, covering the following functions:

  - Store personnel (sales people, backoffice, warehousing, etc.), about 250 heads
  - Creative department, about 30 heads
  - Production and purchase people, 55 heads (in charge of purchasing raw materials, planning and follow up of the production, quality control and so on)
  - CEO and strategies, 20 heads
  - Licensing and sub-contracting, 5 heads
  - Sales people for the wholesale market, 25 heads
  - Finance and accounting, 30 heads
  - Pricing, 5 heads
  - Logistics, 50 heads (including freight forwarding and packaging)
  - Legal, 5 heads
  - Compliance (spread worldwide), 20 heads
  - Taxes and customs, 5 heads

The same company would presumably be present:

- In France for the creative department and strategy and for accessories and leather production
- In Italy for the production of ready-to-wear

- In Switzerland and in the United States for the logistics hubs
- In Japan, China, the United States, France, the United Kingdom, Italy, Middle East, with about 10–15 monobrand stores directly operated by the group.

Of course, our case company, Couture Co., is a 360°-luxury brand and proposes its loyal customers a full range of products:

- Apparels;
- Leather goods and travel products;
- Accessories and small leather goods;
- Perfumes (through third-party licenses);
- Small jewelry products;
- Sun glasses (through third-party licenses);
- Shoes.

The Couture Co. being split into two different lines, main line, showing a proud Couture Co. logo, and a second line, including low entry prices, with denim and other products developed to attract the youngest customer (Couture Co. Young).

The several levels of complexity rising from the management of a relatively small group of companies[4] can be easily streamlined.

2.5 THE ULTIMATE STAGE OF COMPLEXITY – E-SELLING, E-SHOPPING AND LUXURY 2.0[5]

So-called web 2.0 technologies have started to play a leading role in the branding, marketing and commercial strategies of luxury and fashion companies and impose a no-return strategy for both customers and luxury brands.

Until the late 1990s and early 2000s, the market consensus on the potential of new technology and web solutions for the luxury business was nearly non-existent. The analysis of the profile of luxury entrepreneurs was severe and typified by a very conservative and risk-averse business environment. The potential of the Internet for brands and businesses was not recognized.

These attitudes explain the moves made by the majority of luxury brands in the field of e-commerce to launch dedicated, fully owned and monobrand e-stores on fully fledged e-commerce Internet sites. The first players to move from among the main worldwide luxury competitors (Gucci and Armani, for example) only started e-commerce operations some years later, from 2006 to 2007.

The big kick to push luxury brands into the web 2.0 arena was given by some landmark cases, namely Net-a-Porter (www.netaporter.com) and Boo (www.boo.com) that have given a clear picture of the to-do and not-to-do steps, as well as the concrete web 2.0 potential for luxury brands.

Launched in June 2000 by Natalie Massenet, a former magazine journalist and stylist, Net-a-Porter is an online, London-based luxury clothing and accessories e-retailer. The website, presented in the style of a fashion magazine, was launched in 2000 and nowadays stocks over 300 international brands such as Jimmy Choo, Christian Louboutin, Alexander McQueen, Stella McCartney, Givenchy, Marc Jacobs, Chloe and Miu Miu. It ships to 170 countries and offers same-day delivery in London and Manhattan.

Net-a-Porter has successfully established itself as a luxury brand with impeccable packaging and unrivaled customer care and has become the luxury role model for e-retailing.

It now employs more than 500 people in New York City and London and claims to attract over 2 million visitors per month. Thanks to its success and quality (roughly $200 million turnover in 2009), the site was taken over by Richemont, the Swiss luxury goods company, currently the third-largest luxury goods company in the world by turnover, behind LVMH and PPR.

Richemont evaluated the company at $530 million in order to acquire the web 2.0 expertise and to fill the gap of the group in the e-retailing environment.

Our second example produced very different results. Boo.com was a British e-retail company that famously went bust following the dot-com boom of the late 1990s. Boo.com was launched in the autumn of 1999 selling branded fashion apparel over the Internet. The company spent $135 million of venture capital in just 18 months, and it was placed into receivership on 18 May 2000 and liquidated.

The reasons for the failure of Boo provided useful insight into the e-retailing needs of both the customer and the e-retailer.

The first problem was, to a certain extent, unpredictable. It concerned the timing of the launch of the site, which coincided with the dot-com crash.

Sales of Boo.com had grown rapidly, and in the fortnight prior to the site being shut down were around $500,000.

The fundamental problem was that the company had been following an extremely aggressive growth plan, launching simultaneously in multiple European countries.

This plan was founded on the assumption of the ready availability of fresh capital equity investment through the first few years of business until sales caught up with operating expenses. Such capital ceased to be available for all practical purposes in the second quarter of 2000 following dramatic falls in the NASDAQ, presaging the bursting of the dot-com bubble.

Another point of failure concerned the nature of the business itself – the user experience. The boo.com website was widely criticized for being poorly designed for its target audience. The first publicly released version of the site included many heavy pages; for example, the home page was several hundred kilobytes, meaning that many users had to wait minutes for the site to load, as broadband technologies were not widely available at the time.

The complicated design required the site to be displayed in a fixed-size window, which limited the space available to display product information to the customer. Navigation techniques changed as the customer moved around the site. While this appealed to those who were visiting to see the website, it frustrated those who simply wanted to buy clothes.

The site's interface was complex and included a hierarchical system that required the user to answer four or five different questions before sometimes revealing that there were no products in stock in a particular sub-section. The same basic questions then had to be answered again until results were found.

The experiences of the two cases presented above left the luxury world with two conclusions:

1. E-retailing and e-shopping provided a concrete opportunity and market for luxury brands, but

2. E-retailing and e-shopping represented an entirely different business, requiring specific tools and could be successful only if luxury brands put in place specific means.

Following these e-retailing pioneers, several other web 2.0 sites have been successfully launched:

The French site Vente-privee.com, which organizes out-of-season designer brand sales events over a limited period, is available only to members. Founded in 2001, Vente-privee.com now has a database of more than 1 million e-mails, and, in recognition of its concept and business model, received the 'Customer Service of the Year 2010 Award' in two categories: event-based selling and general distance selling.

The Italian company Yoox (the name is said to be composed of the male (Y) and female (X) chromosome letters linked by OO, the symbol of infinity or the "zero" from the binary code) was founded in 2000 and now serves 67 countries worldwide.

The company's concept is to buy up overstock or unsold items from previous seasons directly from renowned fashion houses and sell them online at discounted outlet prices. This enables luxury brands to off-load last year's merchandize without undermining their brands or cannibalizing sales at their existing stores. The concept has developed further with the collaboration of brands and fashion designers who have even created capsule collections specifically for Yoox.com.

Thanks to the Yoox.com experience and leverage, the company developed an in-depth expertise in e-retailing that became a business in itself. Through Yoox Services, it operates the full-price online stores of an impressive list of fashion houses that have decided to move onto web. These include Marni (launched in 2006), Emporio Armani (2007), Diesel (2007), Stone Island (2008), C.P. Company (2008), Valentino SpA (2008), Miss Sixty (2008), Costume National (2008), Energie (2008), Emilio Pucci (2008), Dolce & Gabbana (2009), Moschino (2009), Jil Sander (2009), Dsquared (2009), Bally Shoe (2009), Roberto Cavalli (2009), Napapijri (2010) and Coccinelle (2010), all of which are referred to as 'powered by Yoox'.

Finally, by e-selling luxury brands, Yoox has become a brand in its own right and produces clothing itself and sells it among the other brand names.

The above experiences confirm the relevance of the potential of web 2.0 for the luxury business and also illustrate some of the key factors of the e-business in this sector, such as specificity, customer expectations, technology requirements, product presentation and requirements.

Back in 2007 an article appeared in the *Financial Times* which drew a picture of how many luxury customers there were online:

> A survey of 500 of America's richest families published in 2005 by researchers Doug Harrison and Jim Taylor found that the respondents spent on average 13.7 hours a week online. The Luxury Institute, in a survey of 1000 wealthy consumers published in March, found that 98 per cent used the internet for shopping, and that 88 per cent read product research and review sites.

Today's web-selling environment is even more complex, with leverage from cross-marketing made by global and local social networks, such as Facebook, Twitter, Myspace and virtual communities like Second Life.

Obviously, not all that is found on the net is good content, and putting luxury brands on the Internet can still present risks. Big players have the most at stake, given the energy and money invested in their brands, sometimes over hundreds of years. This said, where there is risk, there is also opportunity. Thankfully, some big brands have recognized this and have started to experiment with some of these new communication channels. Armani and Karl Lagerfeld have brought their fashion show videos to the Internet, iPads, iPods and mobile phones, showing that being a pioneer has nothing to do with age and more to do with attitude. Dior has also experimented with the launch of a jewelry collection on Secondlife.com and several other brands have decided to upload (officially or unofficially) their fashion shows on YouTube.

So now, as with any other business where the product/service becomes commoditized, the key players have to take it to the next level and differentiate themselves in order to keep up with the rapid pace of what is going on. It is not yet a zero sum game because the industry's growth is so high, but with so many players in the game, it is bound to become more competitive. This is where web 2.0 can play a role. Luxury e-commerce sites that differentiate themselves through unique product assortments, clever editorial and content and interactive community development will be the ones to succeed. On the other hand, with retail, it always boils down to number of visits and average purchase size, so it is also important that the interactivity and community do not detract from the primary objective at hand, which is to drive sales.

Web 2.0 is only the latest of the many arenas in which luxury goods multinational enterprises have to fight to impose their prestige and awareness. If they do not, new markets and new customers will flow to competitors and will handicap the players' future – another point of complexity to add to the already complex and diversified luxury arena.

APPENDIX: THE WASHINGTON CONVENTION – CITES

CITES – the Convention on International Trade in Endangered Species of Wild Fauna and Flora – was drafted as a result of a resolution adopted in 1963, and the text of the Convention was finally agreed at a meeting of representatives of 80 countries in Washington DC., USA, on 3 March 1973. CITES came into force on 1 July 1975.

The convention is the milestone of the several steps made by major developed countries to ensure that international trade in wild animals and plants does not threaten their survival.

The use of flora and fauna species for human vanity, to enhance personal status or to affirm power is not a new phenomenon. Animal skins (lions, tigers) and elephant tusks have traditionally been used by tribes to impose their power on other tribes. In modern societies, fur coats, crocodile or python belts and bags, mother of pearl buttons serve a similar purpose.

Two events have led to an increase in the use of such materials. Firstly, the growth of the middle classes possessing an accrued spending power, and, secondly, the new consumerist economy, based on previously unknown production rhythms, and an increased use of flora and fauna components for all sectors of the luxury business, such as fashion, *art de la table*, jewelry and leather goods. This has led to the risk of extinction of several species.

When the ideas for CITES were first formulated in the 1960s, international discussion of the regulation of wildlife trade for conservation purposes was something relatively new and difficult to understand.

Clearly, the cultural element is not the only factor conditioning such a debate, even though today widespread awareness about the endangered status of many species might make the need for such a convention seem obvious. On the other hand, the trade of such protected species provides a business opportunity for many of the poorest countries in the world, primarily in Africa and Asia.

Annually, international wildlife trade is estimated to be worth billions of dollars and includes hundreds of millions of plant and animal specimens. The trade is diverse, ranging from live animals and plants to a vast array of wildlife products derived from them, including food products, exotic leather goods, wooden musical instruments, timber, tourist curios and medicines. Levels of exploitation of some animal and plant species are high and the trade in them, together with other factors, such as habitat loss, can deplete their populations and even bring some species close to extinction.

Thanks to the existence of CITES, the number of wildlife species in trade that are not endangered is limited; however, the existence of an agreement to ensure the sustainability of the trade is fundamental in order to safeguard these resources for the future.

Because the trade in wild animals and plants crosses borders, the effort to regulate it requires international cooperation to safeguard certain species from over-exploitation. CITES was conceived in the spirit of such cooperation. Today, it accords varying degrees of protection to more than 30,000 species of animals and plants, whether they are traded as live specimens, fur coats or dried herbs.

CITES is an international agreement to which states adhere voluntarily. CITES provides a framework to be respected by each participating country which has to adopt its own domestic legislation to ensure that CITES is implemented at the national level.

Since its conception, CITES has found a great international consensus, and today can boast 175 member countries.

3

FINANCE SURVIVAL GUIDE: VALUE CREATION AND *PIÑA COLADAS*

Giulio Pizzini

3.1 INTRODUCTION (*OR WHY BUSINESSES EXIST*)

I hear you sigh, dear reader, as you read the title of this chapter 'Phew, finance, this is boring. Let's quickly skim over these pages and move to marketing, brands and the glitzy lights of the catwalk.'

Let me reassure you that this chapter is not about finance. OK, there will be *some* finance in it, but what we are really going to discuss is the reason why all businesses exist. And how to make you rich, famous and successful.[1]

Before we start, a few words on the approach we will take. We will assume that the reader has no experience whatsoever in Finance or Economics and we will focus on explaining fundamental concepts in a simple and clear way. If you are an experienced CFO looking for the latest wizardry of financial engineering, you are in the wrong place. On the other hand, if you do not even know what a CFO is, keep reading.[2]

Why do businesses exist? To create value for their owners.

Since owners of a company are also called shareholders, value to the owners is typically called shareholder value. In recent times, there has been a lot of debate on whether a company's purpose should really be creating shareholder value instead of creating value in more ample terms to society: its employees, customers, communities and so on.

We will avoid getting entangled in this very complex moral and philosophical issue with a shortcut: we will tacitly agree that for a company to maximize *long-term* shareholder value, it must in fact create value for society, otherwise, for example, its best employees' performances will deteriorate, its customers will stop buying its products, it will be fined by environmental agencies and so on.

So, from now on, we can focus on shareholder value and just call it value. We will also assume that we are all company owners.[3] Yes. All of you, from now on, will think and behave as if the company you work (or will work) for is your own. We know that we want to maximize value, but what do we really mean by value? How do we measure it?

> *What is the value of a company (or an investment, or any business decision)?* Value is the sum of the net, marginal, discounted cash flows generated by the company, investment or decision.

'Discounted cash flows what???' I hear you think.

OK, let's rephrase that: value is the money that the company (or investment, or decision) will put in your pocket (we are the company owners, remember). Simple enough.

But, to calculate how much money will actually end up in your pocket we need to calculate that esoteric sum of future net, marginal, discounted cash flows. I promise you, dear reader, that by the end of this chapter you will know what these mysterious cash flows are. But, before that, we need to build some basic finance foundations, and we will do it with the help of our friend Jack whom you will meet in the next section.

3.2 THE BASICS OF FINANCIAL STATEMENTS (*OR HOW JACK GOT INTO BUSINESS*)

Jack rubbed his eyes and looked out of the window. The sun was slowly rising and the first light of the morning was filtering into his office. He gazed at the clock on the front wall: 5.30am. Not bad for a Monday he grinned – a great way to start the week. He had been up all night trying to understand the financial statements of the first year of operations of his company. 'I should have studied Finance more when I was in school' he sighed.

Jack had graduated one year before from the prestigious SKEMA business school in France, with an MSc in Luxury and Fashion Management. A few months after graduating, he founded his company – Just Jack – and launched his line of luxury shoes for men. The company had grown nicely the first year and Jack had just finished analyzing his financial reports (see Figure 3.1).

BALANCE SHEET at 31 December 2010
Milion Euro

Assets		Liabilties	
Cash	0.3	Payables	0.4
Receivables	1.3	Debt	0.0
Inventory	0.4	Deferred taxes	0.0
Total short-term assets	**2.0**	**Total debt**	**0.4**
Plant, property, equipment	0.4	Initial capital	1.0
Intangibles	0.0	Accumulated earnings	1.0
Total long-term assets	**0.4**	**Total equity**	**2.0**
Total assets	**2.4**	**Total liabilities**	**2.4**

INCOME STATEMENT for 2010
Milion Euro

Sales	5.0
COGS	−1.5
Gross Margin	**3.5**
SG&A	−2.0
EBITDA	**1.5**
Depreciation and amortization	−0.1
EBIT	**1.4**
Interest	0.0
Taxes	−0.4
Net Income	**1.0**

CASH FLOW STATEMENT for 2010
Milion Euro

Net income	1.0
− cash taxes correction	0.0
+ depreciation	0.1
− increase in working capital	−1.3
Cash flow from operations	**−0.2**
New capital investments	−0.5
Cash from disvestitures	0.0
Cash flow from investing	**−0.5**
New capital	1.0
New debt	0.0
Distributions to shareholders	0.0
Cash flow from financing	**1.0**
Total change in cash	**0.3**

FIGURE 3.1 **Just Jack financial statement Year 1**

What do these reports mean? We need to understand what happened to Just Jack and how this translates in financial terms. This is the summary of Just Jack events this year:

1. Jack raised €1.0 M (M stands for millions) from family and outside investors and started the company on 1 January 2010.
2. He invested €0.5 M to open a small shoe production site in Poland (to buy all the equipment needed).
3. He spent €1.5 M during the year on shoe production in his Polish site (buying the leather, paying electricity for the equipment and salaries for the workers....).
4. He spent €1.0 M on renting an office in Paris and paying the salaries of the office staff (a super-efficient assistant, a crazy designer, a marketing genius, a salesperson that never takes no for an answer, a meticulous accountant and himself, of course) and paying the office bills for the year.
5. He spent €1.0 M on promotional events to convince his customers (luxury store owners) to put his shoes in their stores, and the consumers (men with great taste and big wallets) to buy the shoes from the stores.
6. He sold €5.0 M worth of shoes, whoa!

Financial reports have three main components: the balance sheet, the income statement (also called the profit & loss, or P&L) and the statement of cash flows.

The *balance sheet* is a snapshot at a specific moment in time of what the company owns: *assets* like cash, inventory, plants, patents and so on, and what it owes; *liabilities* to third parties or *debt* (money that typically has to be repaid within a fixed timeframe), and liabilities to shareholders or *equity*. You can think about the balance sheet in this way: on the left side you list anything that has value for the company, its assets. The total assets figure represents an accounting measure of value of the company, called *book value*. The right side is always equal to the left side, that is:

$$Assets = Liabilities$$

and it shows how much of the book value of the company can be claimed by third parties (debt) and how much is then left to its owners (equity). Because

$$Assets = Debt + Equity \quad \longrightarrow \quad Equity = Assets - Debt$$

Which is another way of saying that the book value to the owners is the value of all the assets minus the debt that has to be paid.[4]

You are probably asking yourself now what does the book value represent and how does it compare to the actual value of a company. For now, think about it as the value of the company if you were to stop its operations and sell the pieces separately.[5] The actual value of the company represents instead all the future money (cash flows) that it will generate. If you look at public companies (companies listed in the stock market), their traded value is bigger than their book value unless the company is not healthy and investors think that it will lose money in the future and end up losing even the assets it currently owns.

In Figure 3.1, you can see the balance sheet for Just Jack as of 31 December 2010.

The P&L shows what the company earned and spent in a period of time (the whole year 2010 for Just Jack in Figure 3.1) from an *accounting standpoint*. The revenues and expenses in the P&L do not match actual cash in and out in 2010 but all the items that are *pertinent* to 2010. For example, Figure 3.1 shows sales for €5.0 M in 2010, but some of this cash will be paid by the customer in the first few months of 2011 since Just Jack gets paid by its customers only three months after delivery of the goods.

Finally, the *statement of cash flows* shows the actual cash in and out of Just Jack's coffers in 2010.

We will now build the statements together step by step from the events that happened during the year. Let's start from the balance sheet.

On the assets side we have:

- Cash. This shows how much money Just Jack has in the bank, which is €0.3 M. Since the company did not exist one year ago, this means that the net result of all cash in and out during the year was exactly €0.3 M. This number is calculated in detail in the cash flow statement, so we will analyze it later.
- Receivables. This is how much Just Jack still needs to collect from its customers for shoes already sold. Because Just Jack gets paid three months after delivering the goods and it had €5 M in sales

in the year (#6 in the Just Jack event list seen previously) it is still waiting to receive €1.3 M (€5 M over 12 months is €0.4 M per month or €1.3 M for three months).

- Inventory. This is the value of the shoes that Just Jack has produced but not sold yet and is holding in its warehouse. Jack likes to hold a month of sales in inventory to make sure he is never out of shoes for a customer, so his inventory is €0.4 M[6] as we saw above.
- Plant, property and equipment (PPE). This is the value of all physical assets of the company: land, buildings, machines and so on. Just Jack has invested €0.5 M in a building and machines in Poland (#2 in the event list), and this is what we put here. But wait a moment! We only see €0.4 in Figure 3.1! This is because we *depreciate* the value of PPE over time (the machines get older and less valuable), so the number here is the sum of all investments minus all depreciation. We will discuss how to calculate depreciation for the P&L later; for now, the €0.4 M shown here is the difference between the €0.5 M investment and the €0.1 M depreciation found in the P&L.
- Intangibles. Here we would record the value of immaterial (non-physical) assets like patents, brands and so on. Just Jack is a young company and has none of these.

On the liabilities side for debt we have:

- Payables. Just as customers pay Just Jack only after three months; Just Jack pays its own suppliers after three months. The €0.4 M shown here represents what Just Jack still owes to its suppliers for past purchases; it is effectively a debt to suppliers.
- Debt. Just Jack has not borrowed money from banks or other financial institutions and has no other debt.
- Deferred taxes. In most countries, the taxes that are shown in the P&L are not the real taxes paid by the company (also called cash taxes). Based on complicated rules you can learn from somebody else, companies manage to pay fewer taxes in reality than shown by the P&L, and to postpone tax payments in the future. This is a debt to the government and shows up here in the balance sheet. For simplicity, we will assume here that Just Jack cash taxes are equal to the P&L taxes (also called book taxes).

On the liabilities side for equity we have:

- Initial capital. The money put into the company at its inception, in this case €1.0 M (#1 in the event list).
- Accumulated earnings. This is equal to the sum of all the profits made by Just Jack in its history minus all dividends paid to shareholders (all cash given back to the owners). Just Jack made a profit (net income) of €1.0 M that we can see in the P&L and paid no dividends to its owners, so the line on the balance sheet shows €1.0 M.

Now it is time to examine the P&L.

- Sales (or revenues). This is what Just Jack sold in the year or €5.0 M (#6 in the event list).
- COGS (cost of goods sold). How much was spent to produce the goods. This includes the purchase of all raw materials, all production costs and delivery to the customers. It does not include costs related to sales and marketing of the goods, or administration of the company. These we will find in a moment on another line (SG&A for the more impatient readers). For Just Jack this year, COGS was €1.5 M (#3 in the event list).
- Gross margin. The difference between sales and COGS.
- SG&A (sales, general and administration). All the costs that are not production costs. These are all sales and marketing costs, research and development and design costs, and all other administration costs (finance, legal, accounting, human resources, office bills and so on). Just Jack spent €2.0 M on SG&A this year (#4 and #5 in the event list).
- EBITDA (earnings before interest, taxes, depreciation and amortization). The difference between gross margin and SG&A. For mature, stable companies, EBITDA is often close to the actual cash flows of the year and lazy people often simply look up the EBITDA and assume cash flows are the same, which can lead to dramatic mistakes.
- Depreciation and amortization (D&A). The amount of assets that was depreciated in the year. Long-term assets (physical and immaterial) have a depreciation schedule that describes how much to depreciate every year. Just Jack only has €0.5 M worth

of equipment and we think this equipment should last about five years before being too worn out and completely useless, so we depreciate €0.1 M per year (in five years the balance sheet value will be zero and we might really throw the assets away, or maybe not and use them for many more years after all, another reason not to trust the *book value* of a company). Think about the implication of this for a moment: we spent $0.5 M this year but we show in the P&L only a cost of €0.1 M for the year, the rest will be spread over the next four years. Why do we do this?

You will surely remember what we said about the P&L before: it shows revenues and expenses *pertinent* to the year. We did not buy the equipment only for this year but for the next five years of production, so we spread the cost. This means that a company that is showing a positive profit for the year might have actually experienced a negative cash balance if, for instance, it made large investments. While the P&L is the most accurate picture of profitability for the year, managers need to monitor cash flows closely to avoid inadvertently making a profitable company go bankrupt.

- EBIT (earning before interest and taxes). You calculate EBIT as EBITDA minus depreciation. As the name implies, it is the profits before you pay interest on any debt the company might have and taxes.
- Interests. Interests paid on debt: Just Jack has none, so pays no interests.
- Taxes. Companies pay these to help the government provide good services to the people.[7]
- Net income (or net profit). The result of the year that represents how much money was made from activities pertinent to the year.

What were the actual cash flows of Just Jack? You will remember from the balance sheet discussion that we said Just Jack's net cash change amounted to €0.3 M. So how did the €1.0 M in net income translate to only €0.3 M of cash? The cash flow statement shows us the answer.

The statement is divided into three sections:

- Cash flow from operations. This is how much cash was generated by the normal business activities. To build it you start from net income, €1.0 M for Just Jack, and add or subtract three items. The first is the correction in cash taxes if the actual taxes paid were different from the book taxes. For Just Jack they are the same, so this is zero. The second is depreciation that you *add* back to net income since depreciation is an accounting charge and not a real cash outflow (the real cash expense for the machines investment will come in another section of the cash flow statement). The third and last item is the increase in working capital that you need to subtract.

'What is this working capital thing?' you might ask. If you remember, Just Jack gets paid by its customer three months after it sells them shoes. Where does the cash to be utilized to buy raw materials, pay the workers and the bills, and so on come from while the company waits to close sales and get paid? Alternatively, to put it in balance sheet terms, as we book increases in receivables and inventories on the asset side, what do we book on the right side? It has to be cash coming from debt or from owners. Working capital is calculated as receivables + inventory – payables,[8] which for Just Jack is a whopping €1.3 M increase (since last year it was 0 given that the company was not operating yet).

So €1.0 M in net income plus €0.1 M of depreciation minus €1.3 M of working capital increase gives us −€0.2 M of cash flows from operations. Ah, if only customers paid more quickly…

- The next section is cash flow from investing, which is what we spent to buy equipment or other assets netted by any money we made by selling assets. Just Jack invested €0.5 M to start its factory in Poland and did not sell any assets, so the cash flow from investing is −€0.5 M.
- If you sum the cash flow from operations and the cash flow from investing we are now at −€0.7 M. Where did the money to fund this come from? We need to look at the last section of the cash flow statement – the cash flow from financing. Here you add cash

received from debit holders or from shareholders and deduct any repayment of debt or dividends paid back to shareholders. For Just Jack this year the only applicable event was the €1.0 M raised from investors before founding the company, so we book +€1.0 M here.

The total change in cash is then $-0.2 - 0.5 + 1.0 = +0.3$M, which explains how a €1.0 M net income matches an increase in cash of only €0.3 M.

You might be bored to death with financial statements now, so to have some fun I suggest you look up the financial statements of a public company of your choice on the Internet and read them. Some readers might think it would be more fun to take a trip to Mexico and drink *piña colada* on the beach; it is up to you. Just make sure you come back for the next section. You still want to understand how to create value and we are very close to doing it. But first, let's build a small foundation of economics.

3.3 HOW TO THINK LIKE AN ECONOMIST (*OR ONLY WHAT IS MARGINAL REALLY MATTERS*)

Jack shivered a bit as the fresh breeze hit his still wet body. He took a sip from the white glass in his hand and nodded to himself 'Ah, drinking *piña colada* on the beach, much better than pouring over financial data.' Suddenly a young boy kicked his leg, painfully. 'Ola señor!' he shouted happily. Jack rubbed his leg and before he could say anything, the boy snapped, 'You look like a savvy business owner, señor. Let me ask you a question' and he swiftly handed to Jack a crumpled napkin which seemed to materialize out of nowhere with numbers scribbled on it (you can see a reproduction of the napkin in Figure 3.2).

	Product 1	Product 2	Product 3	Product 4	Product 5		Total
Volume	200	100	100	50	50		**500**
Price	€10	€12	€12	€14	€7		
Sales	€2000	€1200	€1200	€700	€350		**€5450**
Cost	€−1600	€−800	€−800	€−400	€−400		**€−4000**
Profit	**€400**	**€400**	**€400**	**€300**	**€−50**		**€1450**

FIGURE 3.2 **Boy's first crumpled napkin**

'Would you stop making Product 5, señor?'

'Well, I think so. I am losing money on it,' said Jack, a bit suspiciously, starting to feel he was being set up.

'Here, have a look at this. There's some more detailed information.' The boy lightly touched Jack's ear and seemed to pull another crumpled napkin out of the ear itself (see Figure 3.3).

Jack started to feel really uncomfortable, certain that the boy was ready to make fun of him 'Uh, I think, well, not...' stammered Jack.

The boy, with an evil grin, put a finger in Jack's nose and seemed to extract a third crumpled napkin (see Figure 3.4).

	Product 1	Product 2	Product 3	Product 4	Product 5	Total
Volume	200	100	100	50	50	**500**
Price	€10	€12	€12	€14	€7	
Sales	€2000	€1200	€1200	€700	€350	**€5450**
Variable cost	€−1200	€−600	€−600	€−300	€−300	**€−3000**
Fixed cost	€−400	€−200	€−200	€−100	€−100	**€−1000**
Profit	**€400**	**€400**	**€400**	**€300**	**€−50**	**€1450**

FIGURE 3.3 **Boy's second crumpled napkin**

A - No action: keep the product

	Product 1	Product 2	Product 3	Product 4	Product 5	Total
Volume	200	100	100	50	50	**500**
Price	€10	€12	€12	€14	€7	
Sales	€2000	€1200	€1200	€700	€350	**€5450**
Variable cost	€−1200	€−600	€−600	€−300	€−300	**€−3000**
Fixed cost	€−400	€−200	€−200	€−100	€−100	**€−1000**
Profit	**€400**	**€400**	**€400**	**€300**	**€−50**	**€1450**

B - Action; stop the product

	Product 1	Product 2	Product 3	Product 4	Product 5	Total
Volume	200	100	100	50		**450**
Price	€10	€12	€12	€14		
Sales	€2000	€1200	€1200	€700	€−	**€5100**
Variable cost	€−1200	€−600	€−600	€ 300	€−	**€−2700**
Fixed cost	€−444	€−222	€−222	€−111	€−	**€−1000**
Profit	**€356**	**€378**	**€378**	**€289**	**€−**	**€1400**

FIGURE 3.4 **Boy's third crumpled napkin**

With a sudden serious look on his face and a pedantic tone that made Jack want to strangle him, the boy started to lecture Jack, 'You need to apply marginal analysis, señor, to make economic decisions. In my example, the fixed costs of the factory would not change if you stopped making product 5 and the fixed costs of product 5 would be reallocated to the other products. They are the rent of the building, the people in the offices, and so on. The best decision is to keep making the product.'

> *What is marginal analysis?* Marginal analysis compares the incremental (marginal) benefits of an action to its incremental (marginal) costs.

Every time you need to make a business or financial decision, you should apply marginal analysis. Marginal analysis is actually very simple to do. You just follow three steps:

1. You project what the results would be if you did not implement the decision you are analyzing. We will call this Schedule A.
2. You project what the results would be if you actually implemented the decision. We will call this Schedule B.
3. You calculate B minus A. This will show you what the marginal result of implementing the decision is.

In our example (Figure 3.4) $B - A = 1400 - 1450 = -€50$, so the marginal impact of the decision is negative and it is a bad decision. This is a rather over-simplified example and in reality you would make marginal analysis simulating a period of time, ten years for example. And because what really matters is value – that is, money in your pocket according to our definition – you need to project cash flows for your marginal analysis, not net income. I know you cannot wait any longer to learn how to do this, but there is one last economic concept we need to learn first: sunk costs.

Assume you have bought an expensive ticket for a very important sports event, so expensive that you had to make a real sacrifice to buy it (for the less sports inclined, imagine a concert, a ballet or any other event you might fancy). When the day of the event comes, you feel sick. You realize that the game will be broadcast on TV and you would really prefer to stay home and watch it lying down on your sofa rather than go out in the cold, the traffic, the big mess of the stadium. But you have paid a lot of money for it and it was a big sacrifice to get the ticket. You hate the idea of wasting all that money. What would you do?

Keep the answer in your mind for now and continue reading about sunk costs.

The definition of sunk costs is very easy:

What are sunk costs? Any cost that has already happened.

Pay attention now: When you do marginal analysis, you never include any sunk costs. Anything that has already happened will not get into your marginal analysis and it is completely irrelevant for any decision regarding future actions. You might think, OK no big deal, but thousands of managers around the world right now are using sunk costs to make decisions. You do not want to be one of them.

Why are sunk costs tricky? Consider the following example. Assume you need to buy new accounting software for your company. You have two options; system A and system B that you think are equally good. System A costs €600, system B costs €500. You would naturally choose system B so you can save €100.

Now imagine a different scenario: you have just bought accounting software for your company for €1000. You then find out that to make the software work properly for your needs you need to spend an additional €600 in customization work. You also find out that you can simply throw away the system you just bought and buy a new system that will also work well for your needs for €500. What do you do?

In theory, it is exactly the same situation as the first scenario: you have an alternative A that costs €600 and an alternative B that costs €500 that is equally good. You should make an easy choice for alternative B. In reality, having spent already €1000 on software A makes some managers choose to keep investing in software A to avoid throwing away the $1000.

When you meet one of these poor fellows, tell them that the $1000 is a sunk cost and thus is completely irrelevant for any future decisions.

By the way, what about the sports event? Would you go to the stadium or stay home? What you paid for the ticket is a sunk cost...

3.4 DISCOUNTED CASH FLOWS (*OR IT IS ALL ABOUT MANAGING RISK*)

We are finally ready to learn to calculate discounted cash flows. Do you remember why we want to do that? The value of a decision is the sum of the marginal discounted cash flows generated by the decision.

Let me ask you a question: Would you prefer me to donate you €100 right now or €100 in one year? Assuming you are sound of mind you would prefer to get your €100 now. Why?

Well, you can say that maybe in one year I will pretend to have forgotten I promised you the money. Or, that inflation will have made the €100 less valuable because you will be able to buy less with it. Or, you can think that you can put the €100 in the bank today and have more than €100 in one year with the interest you will have earned.

So, we all agree that getting €100 in one year is worth less than €100 today. In other words, we need to *discount* the value of a future €100 cash flow to determine its value today.

Consider it the other way round: if you have €100 now, what will be its value in one year? It depends on what you can do with it. For instance, you can put it in the bank and earn 3 percent interest on it, guaranteed with no risk (even if the bank goes bankrupt, the State gives you the money back[9]). You can say that €100 today is worth €103 in one year (100 plus 3% of 100). Conversely, you can say that €103 in one year is worth €100 today.

What if somebody suggests that you give him the €100 instead of putting it in the bank? He will invest it to buy a house (a great bargain he says), renovate it and sell it for a big profit in about a year. He offers to pay back your €100 in a year plus an amount to be negotiated. How much does he need to promise you in one year to make you accept? Obviously more than 3 percent (€103), otherwise you would just put the money in the bank, which is zero risk. Imagine the housing market crashes in the next year (sounds familiar to anyone?) and he cannot resell the house at a profit. You might not even get back the full €100! Depending on how much risk you see in the deal, you will want to earn a rate on your capital of more than 3 percent. If you think the risk is not very high, perhaps 5–10 percent, if it is the end of 2008 and the house is in London, maybe 30 percent.

This rate is called discount rate (or rate of return) and, as discussed, you choose it based on the risk perception of the future cash flows. Once you have determined the discount rate, you can calculate the value of future cash flows with the following formula:

$$FV = PV \times (1 + R)^{\wedge} T \quad \text{or} \quad PV = FV \div (1 + R)^{\wedge} T$$

Where:

- Future value = FV
- Present value = PV
- Discount rate = R
- Number of years = T

So, to calculate the value of €10,000 today in five years at a 3 percent discount rate:

$$€10,000 \times (1 + 3\%)^{\wedge} 5 = €11,593$$

Or, getting €10,000 five years from now valued at a 3 percent discount rate is worth:

$$€10,000 \div (1 + 3\%)^{\wedge} 5 = €8,626$$

Voilà! You have learned to calculate discounted cash flows, I am sure you can hardly contain your excitement now.

The discount rate and the number of years can have a dramatic effect on discounted cash flows. Consider the value of €100,000 in ten years at 3 percent discount rate and compare it to 20 percent discount rate as shown in Figure 3.5 below.

Now that you can calculate discounted cash flows like a Master Jedi, we are ready to measure value. So how do we measure value? Simple. You need to follow these five steps:

1. Choose a forecasting period or for how many years you will forecast cash flows. Typically, this is between 5 and 15 years, based on the duration of the initiative you are looking at.

2. Forecast marginal cash flows year by year for the forecasting period.
3. Choose a terminal value to represent the value of the initiative after the forecasting period is over (more on this later).
4. Choose a discount rate based on the perceived risk of the initiative.
5. Calculate the sum of the discounted cash flows. This is the value of the project, also called NPV (net present value).

We will now go through these steps in more detail using an example. Imagine you own a factory that makes perfume. A new perfume-making technology has become available that is much less energy intensive. Your competitors have adopted the new technology and have slashed prices. You are not able to make profits at the new market prices and forecast that you will lose €15 M per year if you keep the factory open. You can invest €50 M to upgrade your

Discount rate	3%		
Cash flow	**Coming in...**	**Value today**	
€100,000	Today	$= 100{,}000 \div (1{+}3\%)\,\hat{}\,0 =$	€100,000
€100,000	1 year	$= 100{,}000 \div (1{+}3\%)\,\hat{}\,1 =$	€97,087
€100,000	2 years	$= 100{,}000 \div (1{+}3\%)\,\hat{}\,2 =$	€94,260
€100,000	3 years	$= 100{,}000 \div (1{+}3\%)\,\hat{}\,3 =$	€91,514
€100,000	4 years	$= 100{,}000 \div (1{+}3\%)\,\hat{}\,4 =$	€88,849
€100,000	5 years	$= 100{,}000 \div (1{+}3\%)\,\hat{}\,5 =$	€86,261
€100,000	6 years	$= 100{,}000 \div (1{+}3\%)\,\hat{}\,6 =$	€83,748
€100,000	7 years	$= 100{,}000 \div (1{+}3\%)\,\hat{}\,7 =$	€81,309
€100,000	8 years	$= 100{,}000 \div (1{+}3\%)\,\hat{}\,8 =$	€78,941
€100,000	9 years	$= 100{,}000 \div (1{+}3\%)\,\hat{}\,9 =$	€76,642
€100,000	10 years	$= 100{,}000 \div (1{+}3\%)\,\hat{}\,10 =$	**€74,409**

Discount rate	20%		
Cash flow	**Coming in...**	**Value today**	
€100,000	Today	$= 100{,}000 \div (1+20\%)\,\hat{}\,0 =$	€100,000
€100,000	1 year	$= 100{,}000 \div (1+20\%)\,\hat{}\,1 =$	€83,333
€100,000	2 years	$= 100{,}000 \div (1+20\%)\,\hat{}\,2 =$	€69,444
€100,000	3 years	$= 100{,}000 \div (1+20\%)\,\hat{}\,3 =$	€57,870
€100,000	4 years	$= 100{,}000 \div (1+20\%)\,\hat{}\,4 =$	€48,225
€100,000	5 years	$= 100{,}000 \div (1+20\%)\,\hat{}\,5 =$	€40,188
€100,000	6 years	$= 100{,}000 \div (1+20\%)\,\hat{}\,6 =$	€33,490
€100,000	7 years	$= 100{,}000 \div (1+20\%)\,\hat{}\,7 =$	€27,908
€100,000	8 years	$= 100{,}000 \div (1+20\%)\,\hat{}\,8 =$	€23,257
€100,000	9 years	$= 100{,}000 \div (1+20\%)\,\hat{}\,9 =$	€19,381
€100,000	10 years	$= 100{,}000 \div (1+20\%)\,\hat{}\,10 =$	**€16,151**

FIGURE 3.5 **The value of money**

factory's technology and become cost competitive and profitable once more. Do you want to make the investment?

The only way to answer this question is to calculate the value of the investment through marginal analysis (the NPV). We will do this by following the steps above.

1. Forecasting period. We want to match the lifetime of the investment. You know that typically every ten years you need to invest in upgrading your machinery, so we will use ten years.
2. Marginal cash flows. To do marginal cash flows we need to forecast the cash flows if we do *not* make the investment (what we call Schedule A), the cash flows for making the investment (the Schedule B) and calculate B minus A.

What happens if we do not make the investment? The easy answer is we lose €15 M per year. But the easy answer is wrong. Would you really go on losing money year after year forever? No![10] What you would really do is close the factory. This is a critical concept.

Schedule A is not the status quo; it is your best alternative to the investment under consideration.

You do all your analyses and realize that closing down the factory would cost you €15 M (to pay severance to the workers, clean up the site and so on), so your Schedule A cash flows look like those in Figure 3.6.

It is time now to calculate the cash flows for the investment. We learned from the review of the Just Jack financial statements that cash flows have three components: operations, investing and financing (go back to Figure 3.1 to remind yourself how to build cash flows). Imagine that you have projected revenues, cost and so on and have created a P&L and balance sheet forecast (check again Figure 3.1 to remind yourself what a P&L and

A - no investment											
Year	0	1	2	3	4	5	6	7	8	9	10
Cash flows	−15	0	0	0	0	0	0	0	0	0	0
Terminal value											0
Total cash flows	−15	0	0	0	0	0	0	0	0	0	0

FIGURE 3.6 **Schedule A**

balance sheet look like). You can now calculate your cash flows from operations, assuming you get €6 M per year. The cash flow from investing is the €50 M you need initially to upgrade the factory. We will assume that no more investments are needed afterwards.[11] Finally, we will assume that you finance the project from your own money without taking any debt so there are no cash flows from financing. The Schedule B cash flows[12] will then look like those in Figure 3.7.

In 'year 0' (the initial moment of the project) you spend €50 M to upgrade the factory, then every year you get €6 M from operations.

3. Terminal value. My careful reader will have noticed the large terminal value number in year 10: €42 M. We decided to have a forecasted period of ten years. But what happens in year 11? And in year 12? Unless the company goes bankrupt it will continue to generate cash flows in the future. To capture the value of these future cash flows without having to forecast them in eternity we use a terminal value. How can we calculate it? There are different ways to do this, but one is the best one, so we will only learn this one: the terminal value of a project is the market value of the project, or what you can get by selling it. OK, you will say, but how do I know how much I can sell it for? You do this by looking at how much people are buying similar projects today. Typically, companies are sold as at a *multiple* of some financial metrics, like 2 × revenue (revenues times two) or 7 × EBITDA (EBITDA times seven). Companies in the same industry tend to sell for similar multiples calculated on similar financial metrics.[13] So you do some research and understand that perfume factories are typically sold at 7 × EBITDA. Imagine that your P&L forecast shows €6 M EBITDA in year 10, so you put down 7 × 6 = €42 M in year 10 as if we were selling the factory for €42 M.

B - investment											
Year	0	1	2	3	4	5	6	7	8	9	10
Cash flows	−50	6	6	6	6	6	6	6	6	6	6
Terminal value											42
Total cash flows	−50	6	6	6	6	6	6	6	6	6	48

FIGURE 3.7 **Schedule B**

4. Discount rate. Choosing a discount rate is a complex matter and there is no easy formula to use.[14] You want to use a rate that is in line with the return on capital you could get on other projects of comparable risk, so the only way to do this properly is to have accumulated enough experience on investment projects to know what comparable returns are. Imagine you are already very experienced after years of good investments and decide to use 15 percent.
5. We are now ready to calculate the sum of the marginal discounted cash flows (or NPV). Take a look at Figure 3.8.

Do you understand all we are doing in Figure 3.8? Look at the B–A table (the bottom one). The 'total cash flows' line represents the projected marginal cash flows. For year 0 these are $-€35$ M which is $B - A = -50 - (-15) = -35$. Basically, you spend €50 M to upgrade the technology but save the €15 M you would need to close the plant otherwise, so the marginal cost in year 0 is only

A – no investment										
Year	0	1	2	3	4	5	6	7	8	9	10
Cash flows	−15	0	0	0	0	0	0	0	0	0	0
Terminal Value											0
Total Cash flows	−15	0	0	0	0	0	0	0	0	0	0

B – investment										
Year	0	1	2	3	4	5	6	7	8	9	10
Cash flows	−50	6	6	6	6	6	6	6	6	6	6
Terminal Value											42
Total Cash flows	−50	0	6	6	6	6	6	6	6	6	48

B-A; marginal cash flows										
Year	0	1	2	3	4	5	6	7	8	9	10
Cash flows	−35	6	6	6	6	6	6	6	6	6	6
Terminal Value											42
Total Cash flows	−35	6	6	6	6	6	6	6	6	6	48
Discounted cash flow	−35	5	5	4	3	3	3	2	2	2	12
Discounted rate	15%										
NPV	5										
IRR	18%										

FIGURE 3.8 **Projected NPV**

€35 M. After year 1, the marginal cash flows are equal to the Schedule B cash flows since Schedule A cash flows are all zero. The 'discounted cash flows' line represents the cash flow discounted to today's value. For instance, the €48 M in year 10 becomes €12 M using the discounting formula:

$$48 \div (1 + 15\%) \,\hat{}\, 10 = 12$$

The NPV value is nothing other than the simple sum of the all the discounted cash flows. So we get an NPV of €5 M.

Is this good? What if it were zero? Or negative?

A zero NPV project tells you that the project is giving you a return on the money you are spending (your investment) equal to the discount rate you are using. In other words, the project is giving you the same rcturn you would get from other projects of comparable risk. If the project has positive NPV, then the returns are higher than projects of comparable risks, which means you make more money for the same risk. This is a good thing, so you want to do projects that have positive NPV. On the other hand, a project with negative NPV is inferior to projects of comparable risk, which means you are not being compensated fairly for the risk you are taking. This is bad and you do not want to do negative NPV projects.

You will have noticed the IRR number of 18 percent just below the NPV number in Figure 3.8. What is the IRR of a project? IRR stands for 'internal rate of return' and is the discount rate at which the NPV is equal to 0 which represents the return you are making on the project.[15] In this example, you are making €5 M NPV with a discount rate of 15 percent. The IRR of 18 percent tells you that if you were to use 18 percent discount rate for the NPV calculation (instead of 15 percent) the NPV would be zero. Basically, you have a project that gives you a return on investment of 18 percent with a risk comparable to projects that only give you 15 percent return. Life is good.

So now you have your secret receipt to create value: do projects that have positive NPV. Do that long enough and one day, when you are lying on a tropical beach enjoying the fruits of all this value creation, think about how different your life would have been if you hadn't learned Finance. Just don't overdo the *piña coladas*!

4

THE PIER FRAMEWORK OF LUXURY INNOVATION

Jonas Hoffmann and Betina Hoffmann

4.1 INTRODUCTION

Luxury can be described as something exquisite, unique and rare; it is a combination of pleasure and aspiration. Be it a Richard Mille RM 032 Chronograph Diver's Watch, a Montblanc Meisterstück pen, a Hermès Birkin bag or a Ferrari 458 Italia, it is a product[1] that integrates craftsmanship, precious and rare materials, it has roots and it has a soul. It is an object of desire that is refined and positively pleasing.[2] Above all, it represents a dream and gives you prestige.[3] Innovation and creation are the heart of this process. Luxury innovation involves the capacity of someone at a certain moment to integrate unique skills and to sense *l'air du temps* to create something new, unique, an extra-ordinary product or experience.

This chapter explores innovation in the luxury industry. We view innovation as a process comprising four steps: path, insight, excellence in the execution and rareness of experience. We symbolize it by the acronym PIER. Compared to mass markets where finding a *blue ocean* is the target, luxury companies are like a boat sailing the French Riviera aiming to discover a beautiful, exclusive pier in a *calanque*. This pier is a small, private place that in market terms corresponds to a niche to which the company offers unique value and that is able to sustain the company.

This chapter develops these four steps. Innovation happens in a certain moment in a certain place; there are a path and a context.

Examples highlight the interlinked relation between a creator and the environing context. And then it happens: there is an insight. This is a moment well known to those working in the creative industries. This idea should be able to create/shape/meet a market. We revisit here the notion of value proposition in the luxury industry. The passage from the idea to the product is long, and is characterized in the luxury industry by a relentless search for excellence. Finally, the value transfer (purchase or service performance) should be a rare experience involving the client. We finish by exploring how technology and emerging economies will shape luxury innovation in the years to come.

4.2 FRAMEWORK OF LUXURY INNOVATION: PATH

Writing about luxury innovation means talking about exceptional individuals that lived in times and contexts that allowed the emergence of their talent. Take Gabrielle 'Coco' Chanel for example. As a child, she lived for several years in an orphanage in the Cistercian abbey of Aubazine in Corrèze. This rigorous period is said to have inspired her to create 'harmonious clothing with clean lines (like the sober, geometric architecture of the abbey), neutral colors (black and white uniforms as the sisters and residents, beige as the color of the walls) or her logo (the interlaced Cs of the windows in the abbey)'.[4] Other contextual elements include the fact that she started her business during the First World War in a time of fabric shortage that also impacted her style, or the providential appearance of sponsors (like Captain Arthur Edward 'Boy' Capel[5]) at key moments of her business development. Her unique skills and a tremendous work capacity led to the brilliant insights that built Chanel – the reduction of the size of skirts, the use of black (la petite robe noire), the braided tweed suit, the development of fragrances and so on. There is a path: a personal history and a context.

Louis Vuitton was born in 1821 in the department of Jura, France. At the age of 14, he moved to Paris where, three years later, he became an apprentice to a trunk and packing-case-maker. With the arrival of the steam engine which revolutionized transportation and led to the start of international tourism, Louis Vuitton realized the need for innovative and high-quality luggage that could be used aboard the new means of transport – trains and ocean-going ships: the strong, flat, waterproof trunk. Thanks to the quality and craftsmanship of his work, he soon began receiving orders from high-class society and aristocracy. This is when he created his first shop at rue Neuve-des-Capucines in Paris. The later insight to add the LV letters and the monogram (LV symbol) contributed to differentiating the brand, making Louis Vuitton known as the company capable of customizing luggage to serve almost any imaginable purpose. This tradition is the core of the Louis Vuitton brand, and the descendants of Louis Vuitton still manage the division of customized luggage today.[6] We see again the interplay between a creator and his context.

Taking a different perspective, we expose the case of two crafts with a long history in China and India. Chinese porcelain and silk have traveled from China to Europe since Roman times along the Silk Road.[7] Even today, China as a country remains well known for its silk production, but if you want to buy a luxury silk scarf today, where would you go? Probably to a Hermès boutique. As John Kay[8] points out, institutions are a key element to enable some countries to 'get rich'. Among the millions of Chinese working in the silk industry for the last two centuries, is there no one with the skills or intuition of Thierry Hermès and his descendants? This is hard to believe. What is sure is that the economic and political context in China until 30 years ago was unlikely to let a Chinese Thierry Hermès express his potential.

On a similar register, India has a long tradition of gemstone handcraft. The Taj Mahal, built between 1632 and 1648 by Mughal emperor Shah Jahan in memory of his wife Mumtaz Mahal, is a masterpiece of architecture, probably the most beautiful building in the world. As striking as the perfect proportions of the building is the unique use of white marble and precious gemstones in the construction, testimony of exceptional craftsmanship (Figure 4.1).

This craftsmanship finds its center nowadays in the city of Jaipur, capital of Rajasthan. Jaipur was founded in 1727 by Maharaja Sawai Jai Singh II. Early in its history, Jaipur rulers patronized arts and crafts, attracting skilled artisans and craftsmen to the city. Jaipur became the capital of polishing and creation of unique gemstones. And later on, with successive Maharajas, the British Crown became a client of this unique jewellery. Jaipur is estimated to have between

FIGURE 4.1 **Detail of gemstone decoration on the walls of Taj Mahal, India**

200,000 and 300,000 workers involved directly or indirectly in the gemstone trade. Unique companies have come to existence like the Gem Palace or Amrapali.

Could a jeweller from Jaipur today be a global brand as Cartier or Bulgari? Maybe, but the political and economic conditions of the last 150 years have not favored that kind of endeavor (from the British Empire to the relative inward looking nature of India from its independence until the early 1990s). Inspiration and unique craftsmanship were there, but the context, that is, the institutions to allow their global expression, was missing.

History indeed helps explain why luxury industries have emerged in some specific places, like France and Italy. The affluence that characterized the Roman Empire was later revived in the Rinascimento and inspired a tradition of unique design and craftsmanship. The refinement of the French Royalty gave birth to several luxury industries that still exist today: in 1780, Jean-Pierre Clause created the *foie gras* recipe for the Marshal of Contades, who later introduced *foie gras* to the King Louis XVI. Another example is the scented gloves that gave birth to the perfume industry and eventually led Grasse to become the capital of *parfum*.

It is no coincidence that the origins of flagship brands of the main luxury conglomerates are French (Louis Vuitton for LVMH,

Cartier for Richemont) and Italian (Gucci for PPR) origins. And it is the job of entities like the Colbert committee to push regulations in order to protect this context, in this case, *made in France* luxury. We will see later that this is one of the main changes in the years to come, since emerging economies will likely give birth to new codes and meanings that will inevitably change the luxury industry.

One example that will be developed at length in this chapter is the one of Richard Mille. Before launching his own brand in 2001, Richard Mille worked for 27 years in the watch industry. He worked for Mauboussin, Audemars Piguet, Repossi and Baccarat. At the same time, he became involved with the automotive and aviation industries, observing their high-tech mechanical objects. This is the ferment for the development of his watch, Richard Mille.

To sum up, a *path* characterized by the history of an individual and a socio-political-economical context is the departing point for innovation and creation in the luxury industry. However, a path is like the grape vines planted on the unique soil of la *côte d'or* in Burgundy. They could produce grape juice or a bottle of Romanée-Conti. At a certain moment, something happened that made the latter possible.

4.3 FRAMEWORK OF LUXURY INNOVATION: INSIGHT

This is what we call insight, it is the 'eureka', the 'aha' moment. By observing the racing car and aviation industries, Richard Mille had the inspiration to create a performance timepiece. As described by a specialist website, 'Richard Mille timepieces offer a very different conceptual approach in the luxury watch field. It is Mille's goal to be to the watch industry what Ferrari and McLaren are to the automotive field – technologically advanced, innovative and performance oriented. Indeed, the image of Mille is anything but typical. The timepieces produced by this brand are the results of a very talented team of engineers working in an ultra-modern production workshop to serve a strong 21st century concept.'[9]

Boldly, in an industry characterized by a conservative approach, he aims to build tomorrow's watch. In the words of watch industry expert Jacques Molas, 'whereas 98 per cent of the luxury industry uses today's materials to build watches inspired by the 19th century,

Richard Mille uses today's materials (albeit different ones) to build the 21st century watch'. This is the insight: how could we use the high-tech materials of the aviation and automotive industry to build an ultra-performing timepiece? In Richard Mille's words, his concept is based on three pillars:

- the best of the technical developments and innovation applied to the watchmaking industry, inspired from the materials used in aeronautics, Formula 1 and other high-tech sectors;
- the best, in his eyes, of a certain artistic and architectural dimension, and a certain sense of comfort and ergonomics, where performance lies alongside lightness and endurance;
- the best *haute horlogerie* enabled by Swiss fabrication, with handmade craft whatever the cost. The result is all that counts and the cost will be the result of the technical and esthetical choices, and not the process-departing point.

This led to the integration of materials like carbon nanofiber, ALUSIC, Aluminum-Lithium, ANTICORODAL and Phynox, to name a few, in the watchmaking industry.[10]

Richard Mille's insight exemplifies one of the most current approaches in creativity: lateral thinking.[11] Creation and innovation happen at the borders. Insights come when we look at a problem from a different viewpoint. It is influenced by a path, but no path guarantees insight.

The role of the creator is essential, and luxury companies rely heavily on those individuals. Karl Lagerfeld exemplifies this. Starting his career at Pierre Balmain, he later developed an independent career that led him to create collections for brands like Chloe and Fendi. In 1963, he introduced *prêt-à-porter* and accessories for Chloe, and in 1965, he created the Fendi logo. In 1983, he was named artistic director for Chanel's haute couture collections. At that time, Chanel was going through a difficult period following the passing of Coco Chanel in 1971. He rejuvenated the brand, working mainly with the black and white contrasts.[12] He is nowadays a pop symbol as his collections for H&M and his collaboration with *Coke light* attest.

Marc Jacobs is another example. He took the artistic direction at Louis Vuitton in 1997. He has since taken the brand to new grounds, leading the way to the global expansion of Louis Vuitton. His insight to collaborate with Stephen Sprouse to create the graffiti bags, and with Takashi Murakami to develop the multicolored bag, created a new language for Louis Vuitton bags from the traditional brown monogram bag.

On the services sectors, the Marina Bay Casino in Singapore testifies to the insight of building a symbol of the new world. It is the most expensive building (US$ 8 billion) financed by a single man since the building of the pyramids. The architect, Moshe Safdie, boldly incorporated two insights: changing what a casino should look like by 'hiding' the casino in the ground floor and making it a peaceful place, and by building the hanging gardens on the last floor. He planned to unite history and modernity, to anchor a resolute modern place like Singapore with one of the wonders of the ancient world.[13]

This is the fundamental essence of successful luxury products: creating an extra-ordinary product. What is sought is not to delight in a customer-driven 'client is the king' approach, but to push the boundaries of materials and human excellence further in a relentless search for excellence. This is the case of RM 006 and RM 027 watches, built respectively for F1 pilot Felipe Massa and tennis player Rafael Nadal. They were conceived to be used by these sportsmen during competition. Both models had to be exceptionally resistant and ultra-light. RM 006, launched in 2004, used a carbon nanofiber baseplate and was the world's lightest mechanical tourbillon watch with a weight of 48 grams without the strap. According to the brand, it was tested by Felipe Massa during two seasons on the F1 track without chronometric problems. It is Richard Mille's endless search for innovation that has led to insights enabling the development of such products like RM 012 (the first watch with a tubular movement Phynox baseplate), RM 018 'Hommage à Boucheron' (the first watch with wheels created from precious and semi-precious stones) or RM 021 Aerodyne (the first watch created with a composite baseplate utilizing a titanium exterior framework in combination with honeycombed orthorhombic titanium aluminide and carbon nanofiber) (Figure 4.2).[14]

As new materials became a source of inspiration for Richard Mille, the discovery of new stones constituted a special moment in the jewellery industry. This was the case in 1989 when a new

FIGURE 4.2 **Richard Mille watch**

variety of blue tourmaline was discovered in Paraíba, Brazil. This stone became known as Paraíba tourmaline and gave birth to some exquisite collections from the world's most renowned jewellery creators.

An interesting parallel can be found with the design industry where designers' training is mainly about understanding different reference universes to develop a capacity to sense *l'air du temps*. When working with radical new design, customers are not a great help; they are immersed in today's socio-cultural context that shapes their representations and interpretations of meanings.[15] The same goes for luxury creators where a capacity to anticipate new meanings and make a new proposal is a potential source of innovation as shown by Richard Mille, Marc Jacobs and others.

But, being a brilliant creator is not everything. The filing for bankruptcy by Christian Lacroix in 2009 shows that insight does not always lead to a profitable niche. This brings us to the concept of value proposition. The value proposition is the reason why a client pays a certain amount for a product. It is a proposition because it assumes that a product or a service has no inherent value; it just has value when it is acquired by a client. This is a fundamental concept: a manuscript that finds no editor has no market value; a pearl necklace that finds no client has no market value.

Value sources in the luxury industry are predominantly hedonistic (dream) and symbolic (prestige) with a minor role given to the functional value. The esthetics, the pleasure, the social marker value of a product are central, the product being supposed, of course, to also perform the intended function. A Richard Mille wristwatch certainly gives you the time, but wearing an RM 032 is a dream, a source of pleasure, of admiration, of gratification (inner-oriented value), and a sign of association with a certain group and a social statement (other-oriented value). [16] The strategy canvas can be of some help to spot the unique benefits to be created by the company.[17]

Since creators share personality traits with artists, the temptation may be for them to imagine themselves as 'Van Gogh's ahead of their time', that their unique talent is not recognized. That is why we talk about value proposition: a creation has market value if it finds a client. The ability to market a creation is as important as the ability to create it. This is where insight has a double meaning: insight to create a product/service and a market, insight to create and to market. As Andy Warhol stated: 'Being good in business is the most fascinating kind of art. Making money is art and working is art and good business is the best art.'[18]

According to Richard Mille, the business plan of his company was 'traditional and nevertheless radically different! The financial plan was built on an audacious approach in terms of the product and a wise business plan, whereas the opposite is generally observed. The stated goal of the business plan: never be in danger, especially concerning cash-flow, whatever the first sale results are.' This is where Bernard Arnault is remarkable. Branding and marketing are some of the best shared skills in LVMH. Brands are leveraged to a new dimension due to LVMH marketing competence.

4.4 FRAMEWORK OF LUXURY INNOVATION: EXECUTION EXCELLENCE

Transforming an insight into a product is a big jump, and many great ideas fail to concretize either in delivering the promised benefits or in reaching a sustainable market. A central element in the luxury industry is craftsmanship – the human touch. That is what makes a luxury product unique. A luxury product has roots,[19] whether in the manufacture of Ferrari in Maranello (Italy) or the historical atelier of Louis Vuitton luggage in Asnières (France). It is the work of numerous skilled craftsmen that coordinates the production process of a Ferrari, or transforms leather into an exquisite piece of luggage. It is the precision found in Switzerland that makes it the center of luxury watchmaking.

With his insight, Richard Mille worked thousands of hours to develop his watch movement.[20] He then subjected his timepieces to rigorous testing and fine-tuning to get the desired precision and reliability. This eventually led to the RM 001 launched in 2001. Each new model brought a new feature: RM 002 (featuring a titanium plate and function indicator), RM 003 (dual-time indicator) and so on. The components are manufactured from scratch, including screws, pinions, barrel arbor and others. Each movement contains hundreds of components and their production requires more than 20,000 mechanical operations (Figure 4.3).

According to the brand,

> the main elements of the movement – consisting of the escapement, going train and the winding barrel – have been specifically studied and tested to provide optimal shock and thermal resistance. Richard Mille has developed a rapidly rotating winding spring barrel, specially designed to ensure a flat Delta curve response for the power supply to the movement.[21]

As an example, in the execution of RM 027 in collaboration with Rafael Nadal, materials used included a lithium alloy and carbon composite resulting in a movement weighting 3.83 grams and a wristwatch weighting 20 grams including the strap.

Whereas creation has a personal or small team signature, execution holds a collective signature. Richard Mille, for example, works

FIGURE 4.3 **Detail of Richard Mille watch mechanism**

in association with watchmaking companies Renaud & Papi and Audemars Piguet (holding 10 percent shares in Richard Mille). The production of Baccarat crystal ware will involve the crafts of a glass-blower, painter and so on. Chanel N° 5 was created by Gabrielle Chanel in association with *parfumeur* Ernest Beaux and includes 80 ingredients, like jasmine from Grasse, may rose and aldehydes. Combined with its unique flacon, it was an immediate success, a success that continues to this day.

Taking gastronomy as another example, the great insight of Ferran Adrià was to explore food under different states (gas, solid, liquid), but this needs to be translated into a meal to be served at El Bulli. And then needs to be reproduced perfectly day after day. Execution is the capacity of chefs like Alain Ducasse (Louis XV – Monaco), René Redzepi (Noma – Denmark) and Heston Blumenthal (The Fat Duck – England), to transform ingredients that we all can buy in a street market into unforgettable experiences. Where the fish is bought, how it is transformed and finally how it is served will all affect the gastronomic experience.

How is this process managed?[22] The search for excellence is the leading message. Make the ideal bag, make the ideal car. The life span is important – maybe a lifetime; the design should however remain timeless, and this is a tricky equation.[23] It requires complex *savoir-faire*: the French word *métier* is an apt description. It also requires the integration of new manufacturing techniques, what is known as process innovation. The artisan is at the center of this process[24] and the transmission of this *savoir-faire* to apprentices may take years.[25] This transfer process is a good example of tacit knowledge transmission and one of the main challenges ahead lies in the capacity of luxury companies to continuously innovate while keeping their roots, in other words, while maintaining a certain tradition.

The outcome of the execution process is a product or a service with a personality, not a pasteurized mass-market personality, but a unique and exclusive product that is an object of desire and helps to build the client identity, becoming a part of how the client defines him- or herself.

4.5 FRAMEWORK OF LUXURY INNOVATION: RARENESS OF EXPERIENCE

So far, luxury innovation has taken place inside the company, even if some interaction with clients is present. Then comes the moment when the client finally takes possession of the good and the dream materializes. That is when the product is purchased and the service performed, but it extends beyond the purchase act or the service performance. From a client point of view, value is derived each time a luxury product is used, or a service memory emerges. The appreciation of the unique quality of a Patek Philippe watch or a Hermès Kelly bag potentially happens each time the product is used. The souvenir of a stay at Oberoi Amarvilas facing the Taj Mahal may last for a lifetime. Branding has an important role in framing expectations and reassuring clients in this process, as exposed elsewhere in this book.

Managing products and managing services are certainly different, a difference that deserves more consideration than can be given here, but there are some commonalities. The exceptional service performance expected from a stay at the Burj Al Arab hotel in Dubai or from a dinner at Louis XV in Monte-Carlo can be associated with the service level expected at a luxury store. The service should be discrete but perfect. Take a dinner at a Michelin multi-star restaurant: from the appetizer, wine advice, passing to the entrée, first course, second course, cheese choice, dessert and digestive, no *fausse note* is allowed.

The challenges of retailing are developed in another chapter, but it is important to remember that many luxury clients are well informed and passionate about the brand products. A Richard Mille client is likely to have information from sources like the company's website, specialized press, friends and so on. The seller must be knowledgeable and serve as advisor or even more as a concierge. The same applies for luxury stores. As stated by Kapferer and Bastien, 'a luxury product becomes a complete, holistic experience, lived in a multi-sensory manner over time by the client'.[26]

And this is a point where some stores are transforming the luxury shopping experience. Brazil's luxury temple Daslu built its reputation on being a unique spot to be and to be seen in São Paulo. The 17,000-square-meter store is the place to go when in São Paulo: it is a place to meet your acquaintances and almost incidentally buy some items. Daslu is a lifestyle and a social marker. This is in line with Brazilians' use of luxury as a social marker, and it is possible because of an exceptional service level.

Recommendation is a powerful vector of luxury communications and the rare and unique client experience is essential for positive word of mouth. Here comes the sensitive question of point of sales localization. Stores should be located in prestigious locations demanding important logistic and financial means. According to Richard Mille, distribution was developed with an objective of splitting geographical risks, preventing risky concentrations. The brand tries to respect the shipping rule of 'one-third' (1/3 Asia, 1/3 Europe, 1/3 Americas). In 2010, besides the authorized resellers, the company had 13 stores in joint venture. The criterion to become a reseller is to be passionate about representing Richard Mille: watches are technically sophisticated demanding a perfect knowledge of the brand. Richard Mille tries to mix points of sales: for example, generalist resellers (like Montres Prestige in Geneva or Dubail in Paris) are completed by resellers who are specialized in the technical pieces (L'Heure Asch or Chronopassion). The goal is to master the brand progression, by mastering the production, by refusing to give in to the demons of product range extension with 'commercial' models, and by keeping the mean price. It is also about fighting parallel channels and counterfeiting.

The website plays a central role in building the Richard Mille brand image. It is a clear website, respectful of the brand values, communicating the complete product range with high-quality visuals. It also possesses an after-sales interface to enable clients to track, in real time, interventions that may be lengthy due to the model's complexity.

4.6 WHAT IS NEXT IN LUXURY INNOVATION?

Structural changes will continue to transform the luxury industry in the years to come. We may cite the continuous concentration driven by luxury conglomerates, the growing role of Internet as a sales channel and in building brand equity. Concerning luxury innovation, we suggest that the driving forces of technology and globalization are likely to redefine luxury innovation and creation in the future.

Richard Mille's integration of new materials in watchmaking symbolizes the potential of technology to reshape an industry. Similarly, information and communication technologies (ICT) empowered products and services will keep appearing in categories like luxury cars and personal products. An interesting affordance of ICT is instant time knowledge transfer. Analogies and lateral thinking by Richard Mille to integrate car racing and aeronautics materials in the watchmaking industry are likely to be more frequent. ICT also helps to improve the luxury product development from merchandizing, passing by creation, prototyping and production/sourcing.[27]

One potential development is the application of customer knowledge management (CKM)[28] in the luxury sector. Going further than customer relationship management (CRM) systems that integrate knowledge *about* the customer, the goal is to integrate knowledge *from* the client and *for* the client. Using websites as opportunities to educate clients on the use of the product and the brand values is a direct example, but they could be further integrated in being sources of innovation ideas. These clients are passionate and potentially willing to share their insights with their brand. Risks are nevertheless high since the degree of exigency of this client is much higher, but rewards could be enormous in terms of client loyalty. This means going much further than just allowing customers to add their initials and stripes in certain types of handbags and luggage.

Important developments can also be expected in the life sciences aimed at improving human performance (brain implants) and appearance (nanotechnology-based products and procedures), thus bringing medical and esthetical care as markers of luxury consumption. L'Oreal is at the forefront of skin and hair research, DNA sequencing is available and preventive therapies will continue to appear. Luxury products and services are likely to appear on this front. Other technology developments will continue to provide luxury-like experiences, because of their huge initial price: orbital space tourism provided by the Russian Space Agency or sub-orbital space flights offered by Virgin Galactic.

Secondly, globalization in the luxury industry means the dislocation of luxury markets from the economies of the United States, Europe and Japan to emerging economies like China, India, Brazil and Russia. China is expected to become the first market for luxury goods by 2020, with an increase in its share of luxury products consumption from 15 percent to 44 percent.[29] India will represent a luxury market of €10 billions by 2015 according to A.T. Kearney.[30] This process has so far led to the creation of new markets for Western-established luxury brands and the globalization of Western-defined luxury. It is likely, however, that new luxury codes will appear in these countries. Efforts are on the way, like Arab and Indian-defined hospitality, but this goes much further.

A common characteristic of Brazil, India and China is their dynamism and vitality. As these societies become more affluent, it is likely that an increasing number of luxury innovators will appear. To begin with, Western-defined luxury codes may be the rule, but sooner or later luxury codes defined by emerging countries will appear, leading to luxury innovation. China and India both have a long tradition of fine craftsmanship; both countries are kind to their national history and this influence may be a rich source for creating luxury codes. Brazil has a less rich tradition but has an instinctive capacity to break rules, to blend, to mix and to play with codes. This can be a fertile ground for the appearance of Brazilian-defined luxury.

One example of this Brazilian-defined luxury is D.O.M., a restaurant in São Paulo. In 1999, chef Alex Atala created D.O.M. with the aim of creating a 'contemporary restaurant with authorial cuisine bringing back the flavors of Brazilian cookery and discovering new ingredients at the time not much explored, such as açaí, pupunha and cupuaçu'.[31] Since its creation, it has been earning recognition in Brazil and abroad and was ranked seventh in the 2011 S. Pellegrino world's best restaurants. In France, the home of gastronomy, and listed by UNESCO for its intangible cultural heritage, the best-ranked restaurant is ninth (Le Chateaubriand). Putting aside criticism of this kind of ranking, it shows a path that may be seen soon in other luxury sectors: creators blending international standards and local resources will guide innovation. How far these innovators can go in challenging established luxury rules is however an open question.

A continuous understanding of these markets and its education about (Western-defined) luxury consumption is meanwhile a top priority for established groups. In China, for example, incumbents are experimenting with different strategies like developing exhibitions to educate the market (e.g. Chanel),[32] partnering with local creators (Shang Xia and Hermès) or owning local-flavored brands (Shanghai Tang and Richemont). Shanghai Tang advertises itself as 'the only Chinese *haute couture* house with a unique fusion of east meets west silhouettes with exquisite vintage craftsmanship'.[33] In India, Hermès has developed products (e.g. silk) incorporating local trends and has since 2007 partnered with the Khanna family, owners of Oberoi hotels chain. The same applies for Montblanc with the Gandhi collection.

It remains to be seen whether challengers could appear in emerging countries. It is nevertheless certain that luxury creation and innovation will be redefined in the years to come.

4.7 CONCLUSION

Finding a unique and exclusive pier is not easy but is worth the effort. Passion is the secret to luxury innovation. Passion is a distinctive characteristic of luxury innovators in their path; it is the source of insights; and it is passion in the execution and the delivery of a rare experience that will make luxury innovation succeed and sustain brand equity in the long run.

ACKNOWLEDGMENTS

We thank Jacques Molas and Richard Mille. We dedicate this chapter to Diana and Mel.

5

RETAILING IN THE LUXURY INDUSTRY

Alessandro Quintavalle

5.1 INTRODUCTION

The word retail derives from the Old French *retaillier*, which literally means, in tailoring, 'to cut off by hand, clip, and divide'. Although often associated with the sale of goods or merchandize from a fixed location, the etymology explains how retailing refers more to the act of selling goods in individual quantities than the location from which it is sold.

Even though not explicitly part of the original meaning of the word – and therefore not limiting it only to its physical sense – the place where the good is sold is of key importance because it is where the act of purchase takes place and it is also an actual point of contact with the client.

Due to the high symbolic value of their products, luxury brands are in fact, and above all, projects of meaning, which implies that all the related activities, from creation to communication, through logistics, human resources, production and distribution, are expressions of the brand identity.[1]

In addition, the store – physical or virtual – represents the most complete experience for real and virtual brand elements,[2] and in order to finalize a sale, all the manifestations of the brand must be perfectly tuned. As luxury products are by definition non-necessary, even a small error during the act of purchasing would consequently alter the client experience and cancel out all the efforts previously made.

5.2 GLOBALIZATION, DEMOCRATIZATION AND INTERNET: CHALLENGES AND OPPORTUNITIES IN TODAY'S RETAILING

The luxury industry has undergone profound changes over the past 25 years. Socioeconomic and technological factors such as globalization, the rise of the HNWIs (High-Net-Worth Individuals), the democratization of luxury and the introduction of Internet have transformed the segment from niche into a consolidated economic sector whose worth has increased ten times in this short time frame.

One of the factors that have made the leverage of these opportunities possible was the conversion of small family firms into multinational groups. On the one hand, global expansion has meant huge business growth for these groups. On the other, the contemporary need to ensure brand coherence and to deliver similar customer experience in totally different cultures and economies has brought important challenges in distribution and retailing.

Although there is still a debate among academics, practitioners and users about the suitability of the Internet for selling luxury goods, the rise of the Internet has, without question, helped brands in their geographical expansion, initially as a communication tool and then as a retail instrument, thanks to its ability to reach virtually any place in the world.

Recent consumer research has shown how wealthy clients are not only heavy users of the Internet, but also make more online purchases than non-wealthy clients. This trend is even more evident in emerging countries where new generations of rich are growing at a faster rate.[3]

Nonetheless, some doubts are still raised about the suitability of the Internet as a retail channel:

- Luxury brands have always dominated the client relationship by recreating the distance and playing the role of advisor, educator and sociological guide – even to the richest people of this world[4] – whereas the Internet consumer is nowadays in total control of the brand and its messages.[5]
- Online retailing boosts product availability to a mass consumer base whereas the luxury world has always promoted inaccessibility.[6]

- The overexposure of the brand undermines the fragile perception of limited supply of luxury goods[7] and therefore the feeling of desire and exclusivity that are the prerogative of luxury goods.[8]
- The purchasing experience of the luxury store cannot be reproduced online: the lack of physical contact with the product makes it impossible to perfectly reproduce the visuals, smell, touch and feel that are essential for the esthetic appreciation of goods which are sensory in nature.[9]
- The Internet lacks the prestigious locations of the luxury flagship stores.[10]

With regard to this, five considerations are worth noting.

First, luxury today has a new meaning due to the process of democratization that exploded at the end of the 1980s and which allowed many small companies to become the big corporations they are today. A luxury product is no longer only about exclusivity; it is now also about quality, craftsmanship and elegance, and represents values that go beyond the material. Consequently, the relationship between brand and client has changed and the Internet is merely keeping up with the times, in retailing too. Second, information and communication accessibility must not be confused with product accessibility. Although Fabergé's online store can be visited by anyone, the average price of a piece of jewelry carries a €150,000 price tag – not one that could be regarded as accessible. Third, the accessibility of information is not necessarily negative in luxury. The purchase experience has two dimensions: personal and social, respectively, defined by Kapferer as 'luxury for oneself' and 'luxury for others'. The first dimension is associated with the personal pleasure in acquiring the object. The second is associated more with public recognition. Therefore, as more people become familiar with the brand, the more pleasant the social facet will be. It goes without saying that in luxury, it is necessary not only to communicate to your target, but also to reach the non-target. This is quite different from what happens in other sectors. In 1995, Dubois and Paternault developed a formula called the 'dream equation' to explain this concept by linking awareness, purchase and dream value to explain luxury where[11]

$$DREAM = -8.6 + 0.58 \text{ AWARENESS} - 0.59 \text{ PURCHASE}$$

According to the authors, in luxury, the purchase destroys the dream because it carries away a portion of dream with the product. But, what is even more relevant is that without awareness, there is no dream. Consequently, the dream must constantly be recreated by making more people aware of the brand than those who can actually afford it. And Internet provides a great opportunity; not only to expand sales, but also to spread the awareness of a brand globally, with definitely lower costs than any offline option.

Fourth, technology has made such progress that the online purchasing experience is getting closer to that of the offline experience, as will be shown later. Finally, rather than looking for perfect reproduction, it is worth focusing on the advantages that e-retailing offers over traditional purchasing: accessibility 24 hours a day, and 365 days a year (key for the busy lifestyles of the HNWIs), more intimate and totally controlled shopping experience (the client looks for advice only when desired).

While online sales have, so far, not taken up offline sales, and while there are still some types of products that need after-sales and store support due to their technical complexity (certain luxury watches, for example), online sales can no longer be considered an appendix of offline. For many luxury brands that have successfully implemented e-retail, it is one of their fastest growing distribution channels.[12]

For this reason, each topic in the chapter will be presented in a dual online/offline format, with the aim of showing that the differences between these two channels are smaller than generally thought.

5.3 LUXURY RETAIL DESIGN

The store is undoubtedly the most powerful communication tool of a luxury brand because it acts as showcase for the product while simultaneously offering the customer an interactive and multisensory experience.

The product is, on the other hand, the most effective and important manifestation of the brand identity since it represents both its ethics and esthetics: it not only directly advertises the physical, but it also expresses the values, the *savoir-faire,* the research and creativity on which the brand has established its legitimacy in a specific sector.[13]

In a store, customers receive a luxury service and experience the brand through the building, architecture, music, odors, decoration, light, logos and esthetics of the staff.

The luxury store forms an integral part of the brand, presenting it as a whole. This is why design is considered of primary importance in retailing, and why the same concepts and atmosphere are normally applied to every boutique around the world, to create the same customer experience.

The goal of the store is to present the luxury product as an *objet d'art*, a factor which explains the frequent involvement of prestigious designers and architects who show the intimate relationship between luxury and art, and how luxury brands are promoters of culture and esthetic trends.[14]

Although the Internet lacks the physical dimension of the brand, online luxury stores can play an important role in increasing the brand and purchasing experience. The significant progress made over the past years testifies just to what extent e-boutique design is catalyzing attention.

French consultants Luxe Corp coined the term Luxemosphere® to describe the atmosphere that a luxury brand's website aims to create online and offline. Specifically, luxemosphere developed from the concept of webmosphere – the reproduction of five senses in a website – because it aims to replicate online the signatures and codes that are used offline by a luxury brand to characterize its unique identity.

Thanks to digital technologies that work on the mind rather than the eye, luxemosphere influences the senses, stimulates the mood and creates emotions so that clients love and respect the brand in the way they do when visiting a physical store.[15]

5.3.1 Offline boutique design

As well as being a physical place of sale, the store is also a communication tool and, not surprisingly, its effectiveness is measured with similar metrics as those used for advertising (with which there must be a coherence in terms of style and codes). Some luxury brands in fact consider the number of people entering the store a measure comparable to the cost per contact.[16]

The elegance and sophistication of a boutique must communicate the price level of the product to be sold yet should not discourage potential customers from entering.[17] On the contrary, a boutique should be designed so that people want to stay as long as possible and purchase the goods.

(a) Location

In contrast to the mass market, where the choice of the location is driven by socio-economic factors including traffic-flow and income, in luxury, prestige is the key factor: the presence in important locations is strategic in communicating the brand's positioning and personality, toward competitors too. Size is of course important to affirm the brand's strength, but in terms of equity creation, for the same rental costs, the combination smaller-size/better-location seems to work better than the inverse. The closeness of two stores of equal prestige is not a negative factor. In fact, it reinforces the images of both, since each brand has its own universe, which is not in competition with any other *maison*.[18]

(b) Layout

The free-flow design and the loop are two of the most popular layout schemes used in luxury boutiques although the final choice depends on the category of goods and on the distribution format. Given the same brand, a flagship must differ, for instance, from a duty-free store because the objectives and the type of interaction with the clients are different.[19]

The circulating patterns are also designed to encourage the independence during the visit so that clients do not feel any pressure from the staff members; these tactics – known as impersonal selling – still have sales maximization as their ultimate goal. Design of multifloor stores is based on the right trade-off between accessibility and exclusivity, by gradually assigning the most prestigious product lines to the upper floors.[20]

(c) Multisensory experience

Luxury retailing aims to immerse clients in a multisensory experience that generates positive emotions, so that the first visit to the store is remembered and the brand perception is influenced accordingly.

These are the tactics applied to each of the senses to create an attractive atmosphere:[21]

- *Sight*: The visual aspect is influenced by
    a. *Color*: Effective use of chromatic tones in keeping with the brand's identity in the representations differentiates areas of the store and influences the perception of the spaces and volumes
    b. *Lighting*: It influences the perception of shapes and volumes and helps to enhance the characteristics of the displayed product
    c. *Size*: It is the statement of the brand's power. High roofs help the presentation and lend more importance to the product
    d. *Decoration*: The luxury store is a projection of the art and the expertise of the brand and the use of video screens, displays and wall mounts reinforces its message.

- *Hearing*: It is part of the environment and should be complementary to both the brand personality and the purchasing act by accompanying and not disturbing the client. Rather than using prepared soundtracks, music should be chosen according to the target public.

- *Touch*: Allowing consumers to feel the luxury product before purchasing it is fundamental. The accessibility of this may vary and be more or less direct according to the type of goods and the intrinsic level of exclusivity.

- *Smell*: It is important for enriching the store experience, fundamental when the brand has extended its range into fragrances and cosmetics; needless to say, coherence and resonance are mandatory.

- *Taste*: When the brand has not yet included food products in its range (fine wines and chocolates, for example), a tactic for enhancing this sense is to include a tasting experience in the event the brand organizes.

(d) Merchandizing

Merchandizing techniques have the important role of pushing the products into the market while finding a compromise between apparently opposite needs. Although it is important to maximize the profitability per square meter, it is clear that a luxury boutique must avoid appearing like a supermarket, so there should be no unnecessary duplication of windows and displays. By the same token, issues of stocking should not affect the client experience either. The product is in fact the star and, as already said, it is the most important manifestation of the brand. It should be displayed as the king but a very low product density in the store may, on the contrary, produce a feeling of poorness and astaticism. One way to overcome this problem is to frequently renew windows and displays, so that clients are invited to visit the point of sale more often.

Low density of products has been traditionally associated with a high price level and items displayed in a spacious glass case imply luxury.

Other merchandizing techniques include pricing and ticketing display, product packaging, point-of-sale advertising and product hot spots.

CASE STUDY 5.3A

Located in via Montenapoleone, the most famous street of Milan located and in the heart of the Luxury District, it is the first ever Rolex Flagship Store in Europe. It was designed by architect Claudio Monti in collaboration with Rolex Geneva interior design team and hosted in a specially restored liberty-style palace dating from the beginning of the twentieth century.

The store has a surface area of 400 square meters, developed over 5 floors. The first floor is dedicated to sales, the second hosts the technical assistance center with four skilled watchmakers and the top floor is a garden terrace dedicated to ad-hoc exhibitions and special events such as dinners with top chefs.

In designing the ambiance, architects have associated the color green – the corporate color of Rolex – with its deeper association with the environment and have developed the project around the concept of a highly livable space, where nature, green and light combine to provide an elevated sense of well-being and quality of life.

FIGURE 5.1 **Rolex Flagship Store, Milan**

Crossing the threshold of the Rolex Flagship Store one sees a panoramic glass lift and in the background the vertical garden, conceived by the French botanist landscaper Patrick Blanc, made of 3500 species of fern and climbing plants (Figure 5.1).

This concept of 'oasis in the urban chaos' is completed with interiors using the finest materials that suit the coordinated elegant and sporty image of the brand while creating a warm and enveloping environment. This 'wall of greenery' can be seen from every corner of the interior space and is marked by the sculptural staircase made from Tanganyika wood that creates smooth and sinuous ramps. The ground floor features a six-meter sales counter made of 'aqua glass', in perfect resonance with the liquidity of the sea, a long-standing emblem of the Rolex brand. On the opposite side is a four-per-nine wall in beige leather sporting the 'Jubilee' logo.

The exterior windows feature mosaic tiles reproducing details from Milan Cathedral (Duomo) and big LCD screens that work as digital book showcasing images of the products and the Rolex world such as cultural and sports events sponsored by the brand.

Finally, the atmospheric quality is created by careful soundproofing and lighting, diffused by the special fixtures designed by Erco.

5.3.2 Online boutique design

A luxury e-boutique should offer the same full experience of a brick-and-mortar format and, without exception, guide the visitor toward the full discovery of the brand. In addition to brochures, catalogs and full product descriptions, information about the know-how, history, achievements, events, initiatives, brand philosophy, values and beliefs should be available.

As a general approach, two guidelines must be considered when designing a luxury e-boutique:

1. *Concept*: The model of website chosen for creating a compelling online atmosphere and driving the choice of all the website elements such as layout, colors, navigation and so on.[22]
2. *Design coherence*: The esthetics and ethics should be perfectly linked with the concept throughout the website.

In perfect analogy with the previous section, the elements of the design of an online boutique will now be presented, showing once again how these two dimensions are conceptually almost identical and do not constitute two separate worlds.

(a) Location
    The Internet is a world available to the masses and it does not match the prerogatives of exclusivity and inaccessibility of the luxury world as everybody has the same opportunity to access a website regardless of personal income and social status. Nonetheless, luxury brands have an opportunity to stand out from the masses by creating a powerful website with a prestigious online atmosphere far removed from the mass contents. After all, even the physical flagship stores are open to everybody, but they suggest distance and inaccessibility through careful design and upscale location.
(b) Layout
    Another feature that should distinguish a luxury from a general website is the presence of a welcome page.[23] The welcome page forms part of the e-boutique like the entry door of a prestigious physical retail location, that is to say, it allows access to the

universe of the brand, and it has a different function from that of the home page.

Once inside the brand world, it is important to do everything possible to make the client feel at ease, discover everything about the brand – the product in particular – and of course finalize the visit with a purchase. A user-friendly classification of products and breadcrumbs[24] to quickly remember the path followed from the entrance are, for instance, one of the two most important tools.

(c) Multisensory experience (ambiance)

- *Sight*: The visual aspect is influenced by
  a. *Color*: It should be linked to the brand's color yet favor, where possible, a white background to distinguish the texts in dark colors. The font should also match the brand personality.
  b. *Size*: An impressive home page is comparable to the ground floor of a luxury boutique, hence the importance of leaving the right first impression.
  c. *Decoration*: Images help communicate the brand identity, yet they must be fitted into the right environment, and a proper display welcomes a luxury product.

- *Hearing*: As in the offline boutique, music must be coherent with the brand personality (preferably ad-hoc composed) and different melodies may feature in different sections of the website.[25]

- *Touch*: The tactile sense cannot be fully reproduced online yet it can be stimulated using video, 3-D views, multiple-size zoom and flipping pages to suggest movement and association with touch.

- *Smell*: The reproduction of scent is one of the other challenges of online multisensory experience even if digital scents have been recently developed, so that a sequence of notes emitted by computer devices reproduces the same effect of a smell.[26]

- *Taste*: Although not possible to have online visitors taste products, detailed descriptions of its taste or videos and images of people tasting the product act as very powerful evocative techniques to render the same effect.[27]

(d) Merchandizing

Methods used online for pushing the products into the market are mainly of an interactive nature. The most advanced are:

■ *Visuals*: 3-D views, zoom, product color selection.
■ *Direct interaction*: Direct interaction with the brand through chat, telephone and video assisting the shopping experience 24/7.
■ *Augmented reality*: It is defined as interactive, real-time and 3D combination of real and virtual elements.[28] Augmented reality gives the web visitor the opportunity to try on products virtually in the form of computer/telephone applications and shows how a jewel, watch, dress or even make up would appear if worn or used by the potential customer. Noteworthy examples are the Girard-Perregaux application for watches or the microsite myboucheron.com.

CASE ANALYSIS 5.3B: THE WATCH AVENUE

Pioneered by the Editions Temps International, gathering a group of top Swiss watch manufacturers (Vacheron Constantin, Piaget, Audemars Piguet to name a few), the Watch Avenue is an unprecedented concept of immersive virtual 3-D in the watchmaking world where visitors enjoy a full journey through interactive features that replicate a real luxury experience (Figure 5.2).

Although designed for communication purposes – retail is currently not available – this website is a breakthrough in terms of how an e-boutique can deliver a superb branding experience in the virtual world, since it overcomes some of the limits – and even misconceptions – of luxury e-retail, specifically the lack of:

(a) an exclusive and prestigious location
(b) the physical retail store
(c) the interaction with real salespeople.

The exclusive location is reproduced through a concept of a virtual luxury shopping avenue where the visitor can find a series of monobrand watch boutiques surrounded by all the characteristics of a high-end district such as trees, street signs, lamps, fountains

FIGURE 5.2 **The Watch Avenue**

and flying birds. To bring a touch of prestige, a young woman escorts the visitors in perfect concierge style in their journey along the two streets of the city, First Avenue and Second Avenue.

The design of the individual stores – both interior and exterior – is in keeping with the identity of each brand: Hublot communicates its 'Technology Fusion' motif with images and videos of sophisticated watch mechanism on black walls and floors, whereas Piaget stands for a refined elegance that is second to none. The sophisticated ambience is obtained using 3-D images of real boutiques, televisions displaying videos and images, real sounds instead of music and a sheer rather than sumptuous design style. Once inside, the user has access to a complete overview of the brand: history, product collections, press releases and technical information about the mechanisms.

The interaction with real salespeople is introduced with realistic simulated figures who welcome the users at the front door – each boutique has a different salesperson – and assist them during the visit, thanks to a help-on-click modality.

Luxury brands are above all relational brands, that is to say they promote, through the product, an exchange – physical and symbolic – between the consumer and producer. As the retail location is one of the main places where this interaction takes place, the Watch Avenue has every element that could enhance the relational side of the experience:

- a cinema broadcasting commercials, news and videos on fine timepieces
- e-Watches, official website of The Watch Avenue as well as blog offering the most updated news on events, people, brands and product introduction of the horological world, a bookstore proposing books about fine watches and jewelry
- a bookstore proposing books about fine watches and jewelry
- the Watchmaking School of Geneva where a personable professor answers questions about watches
- a Virtual Gallery presenting images loaned by three of the most important European museums of photography, to accentuate the connection between two professions that unite craft and creation, art and technology
- The Tag Heuer Museum.

5.4 DISTRIBUTION FORMATS

The retail formats used in the luxury industry can be classified according to two variables:

- Channel: indicating the level of control operated by the brand (this can be direct or indirect)
- Typology: addressing the several goals that retailing covers within the strategy of a luxury brand (revenue generation, client loyalty, market intelligence, communication)

The ideal model is represented by the brand owning, managing and selling exclusively through its own shops. This ensures complete control of image, stock, pricing, client experience, brand communication and protection.[29] To be economically viable, this solution requires a strong power. Therefore, with the exception of a few cases such as Louis Vuitton and Hermès having exclusively monobrand stores, almost all the luxury houses rely on a mixed system which has anyway to reflect the core strategy.

Below is a chart summarizing all the types of formats currently used, further divided into offline and online (Table 5.1).

5.4.1 Offline distribution formats

(a) Directly operated

- *Flagship stores*: Characterized by a wide exposure area, located in the most prestigious area and with a wide range of the

TABLE 5.1 **Distribution formats**

	Offline	**Online**
Direct	• Flagship stores • Monobrand selling points • Shop-in-shop • Factory outlet center (F.O.C) • Temporary store	• Flagship E-store • Monobrand E-boutique • E-commerce integrated website • Online monobrand outlet
Indirect	• Multibrand sales point • Department stores • Corner • Duty-free shop • Franchising network	• Multibrand online store • Online department store • Corner • Pure e-discounters

brand products, including unique and highly specialized pieces granting full mark ups and profits. The main goals are customer communication, evocation of brand values, and maximization of product visibility. Due to the strategic importance in terms of image, they are generally not tied by turnover bonds (they may even have negative financial ROI). Payment of key money (access fee)[30] is sometimes necessary to enter a prestigious location (Table 5.2).

■ *Monobrand selling points*: Located in main tourist areas and major cities, characterized by smaller selling areas and lower realization costs, they are affordable not only to big brands but also to small and medium enterprises. The main goal is market coverage and turnover maximization (profitability per square meter is higher than in flagship stores) as well as the collection of market and customer information.

■ *Shop-in-shop*: Monobrand point of smaller selling areas located inside multibrand department stores; layout and atmosphere are the same worldwide to offer the same brand experience; and full product range is generally displayed. Management, logistics and staff costs are covered by the company owning the brand.

■ *Factory outlet center (F.O.C)*: Characterized by a wide exposure area and several directly managed monobrand boutiques offering unsold and damaged products, items of the previous season or out of production, collections of samples, end of collection models or from fairs and exhibitions, and second-choice products. Discounts range from 30 up to 70 percent of the original price, and customer experience and level of service are coherent with the standards brand – the staff belongs to the producer. These centers are generally located outside cities but equidistant from two or

TABLE 5.2 **The most prestigious streets in the world**

Fifth Avenue (New York)	Place Vendôme (Paris)	Bond Street (London)
Soho (New York)	Avenue Montaigne (Paris)	Calle Serrano (Madrid)
57th Avenue (New York)	Champs Elysees (Paris)	Omotesando (Tokyo)
Rodeo Drive (Los Angeles)	Via Montenapoleone (Milan)	Ginza (Tokyo)

more urban conglomerates. This choice is driven both by socio-demographic logics (target market potential) and by the need to protect the brand. Discounting is in fact operated in a controlled environment and preserves the core target of clients, while at the same time experimenting with new products and types of customers.

■ *Temporary store*: Selling point opened and directly managed by the brand for a limited time period – sometimes to replace flagship stores during restoration while maintaining revenues – and whose goal is to engage the consumer, communicate the values, reinforce the brand image and create a sense of exclusivity.

(b) Indirectly operated

■ *Multibrand sales point*: Intermediary for either a type of product or a target consumer. It features a wide range of selected brands positioned on higher-level prices. Its strengths are the specialization of the assortment, the high level of customer service, the well-established image in the area. Due to the relationship of trust, loyalty and closeness to the consumers, directors of multibrand sales points are often consulted as opinion leaders on market trends.

■ *Department stores*: Characterized by a large surface in which premium price brands cohabit with private labels with an accessible offer, and established in the main streets of towns despite their notable size. They display products in various areas under concessions. Able to exploit the attraction of brands with highly symbolic values, department stores obtain an advantage in terms of lower investments in communication to reach their customers. Famous examples are, to name a few, Harrods and Selfridges in London, Galleries Lafayette in Paris and the store chains Neimann Marcus and Saks Fifth Avenue in the United States.

■ *Dedicated space or corner*: Exposition area open to the consumer where the offer of one specific brand displayed is related to one available space. Assortment and atmosphere are the responsibility of the brand while the sales personnel is sponsored by the storeowner. A convenient format for small and medium enterprises thanks to the high distribution coverage available at low fixed costs while maintaining an unaltered brand image.

- *Duty-free shop*: Intermediary situated in transit areas such as airports, large train stations, arrival and departure terminals of cruise ships. It is an interesting channel for conquering the occasional and the traditional consumers who travel for work and may have idle time to use in browsing and watching. Due to the internationality of the prospect, it is key to develop the same atmosphere, concept and visual merchandizing throughout the world.

- *Franchising network*: A franchising relationship occurs when a *franchisor* company grants to another company – the franchisee – in exchange for sales royalties the right to use its own commercial formula and/or know-how within a defined geographical area in accordance with defined regulations and with a given sign or brand. Suitable when a company brand needs to:

   – Reach the potential costumers in a more capillary way without additional costs
   – Quickly penetrate a new market
   – Need to expand abroad without sustaining the costs of setting up a direct network
   – Develop activities, assistance and relations with the customer in a local context.

The franchisor acts as a channel leader by dictating commercial policies to the franchisees who, on the other hand, take full advantage by benefiting from the already established loyalty of the consumers to the brand.

CASE STUDY 5.4A: PISA OROLOGERIA

Perfectly interpreting the needs of a continually more expert and demanding public, Pisa Orologeria – one of the most important European top-end watch retailers – set, in 2008, a precedent in the way fine watches are presented and sold by introducing a format featuring the advantages of a directly owned boutique – totally dedicated brand experience – with those of a specialized multibrand boutique – experience and consolidated relationship with local clientele.

During the same year, Pisa Orologeria unveiled:

■ **The Multi-Brand Pisa Boutique**, subsequent to the complete restructuring and enlargement of the historical site of Via Verri in the heart of the luxury district in Milan.
■ **The first Rolex Flagship Store in Europe**, in the close by Via Montenapoleone.
■ **The Patek Philippe Space**, also in Via Verri.

The Multi-Brand Pisa Boutique, which features a circular entrance with imposing windows and with interiors studied to favor calm and privacy, not only showcases the models of the large horological groups (Richemont, Swatch, LVMH), the renowned independent brands and the single Master-Watchmakers, but has also a dedicated space for Vacheron Constantin, called the Dream Room.

The *Spazio Patek Philippe* is a completely new boutique that reflects the philosophy of the brand and its ties with tradition and innovations, a space with the same level of excellence as the timepieces from Geneva and where the clients feel at ease, take time, receive information regarding the new items and techniques before making their purchase. The Rolex and Patek Philippe projects have both been designed and started up under the sponsorship of Pisa Orologeria, in close collaboration with the top management of the two prestigious Swiss manufacturers, and they certainly do not represent separate initiatives. Rolex and Patek are respectively the first and second independent top selling brands in the world. They both avail themselves of an internal production cycle, they are not distribution oriented – very few boutiques in the world – and are regarded by aficionados as two non-antithetical ways of expressing top watchmaking (Figure 5.3).

5.4.2 Online distribution formats

Although approached very carefully by managers of luxury brands, e-retail offers several advantages ranging from a direct relationship

Multibrand sales boutique (Pisa multibrand point)

Flagship store   Dedicated space: (Vacheron Constantin dream
(Rolex)   room)

Monobrand selling point (Patek Philippe)

FIGURE 5.3 **Pisa Orologeria, top Italian high-end watch retailer, deploys a commercial strategy with four different distribution formats**

with customers (market intelligence), protection of the brand from non-official offers, availability of new consumers in geographic areas not covered by resellers and the possibility to make purchases

24 hours a day, 7 days a week. As further proof of the validity of this channel, there is also a clear similarity between online and offline formats.

(a) Directly operated

- *Flagship e-store*: Online shop acting for the brand as the main and most complete selling point, possibly the only one available, such as in the case of the jeweler Fabergé, who bet more on the digital than the bricks and mortar solution.
- *Monobrand e-boutique*: Website of a brand dedicated to e-commerce and separated by the corporate website. Worthy of note are the cases of Tag Heuer with Tagheuereboutique.com, where the brand sells eyewear, leather goods and accessories directly to consumers, and the Yoox Group which manages the digital boutiques of Emporio Armani, Valentino and Roberto Cavalli and other important *griffes*.
- *E-commerce integrated website*: Corporate websites of luxury brands with enabled e-commerce functionalities. Examples of this format are Tiffany (diamonds up to US$6 million), Hermès and Bell & Ross (first high-end watch manufacturer to make its full collection available online). One of the latest developments is represented by F-commerce (Facebook commerce) – which is normally integrated to the brand website through an application. An excellent case is the Bulgari Enchanted Garden application which provides the links to the brand's e-commerce site and its commerce section on Facebook and allows the consumers to purchase either way indifferently.[31]
- *Online monobrand outlet*: Some brands have microsites or pages of their websites dedicated to discounted products. This practice is more common in premium fashion brands than in pure luxury brands, which generally do not declare it and opt instead for more discrete ways of clearing unsold items: the perfect luxury product should in fact be timelessness, a concept that is antithetic to that of obsolescence called on by price reduction.[32]

(b) Indirectly operated

- *Multibrand online store*: Like its offline counterpart, it stands for the specialization of its assortment and the range of highly positioned brands. Examples include retailers that also have a bricks and mortar presence (e.g. Patek Philippe official retailers Mappin & Webb in the United Kingdom and Hamilton Jewelers London, Jewelers in the United States) or are exclusively online.

- *Online department store*: It can be exclusively online (Net-a-Porter, full-price sales of luxury fashion items of the current season) or integrate the offline business (Harrods). Other typologies of online department stores may be considered – the virtual shopping streets, platforms allowing users to virtually visit a luxury district populated by interactive monobrand boutiques that act *de facto* as shop-in-shops. Among the most famous, the previously presented The Watch Avenue and The Cosmopolitan Boulevard application.[33]

- *Dedicated e-space or e-corner*: www.thecorner.com is – as its name suggests – a virtual space presenting a broad selection of cutting-edge and superior craftsmanship products and where each brand has a dedicated microstore (corner). By showing articles, reviews, pictures of the collections and exclusive videos, each name can promote its offer in full coherence with its DNA and values.

- *Online outlet*: Pure internet player competing on prices, where goods are available with discounts of up to 70 percent. Venteprivée.com and Outnet.com are among the most famous.

CASE STUDY 5.4B: FABERGÉ

Fabergé, the brand of high jewelry and ornamental pieces founded in 1885 by Peter Carl, was relaunched in September 2009 after 93 years of inactivity. This return attracted a lot of attention not only for the prestige of the name (Fabergé was known as the 'Jeweler of the Tsars') but also for the innovative retailing format proposed: for the first time an ultra-luxury brand made its debut exclusively through an online flagship store. In December 2009, a physical store was opened in Geneva but the online is intended to remain the main interface with the clients, with the offline being the place where the whole collections are kept.

The goal of the online flagship store is to create an ultimately exclusive and intimate relationship between the client, the pieces and the salespeople of the House, with a level of service comparable to that of VIP private selling, thanks to a highly interactive technology.

According to the CEO, Mark Dunhill, 'it would take 10 years to start up a network of stores and stock them with expensive inventory'. In addition to that, the relaunched jewelry house will avoid advertising so as not to introduce risk, but it will focus instead on the strength of this innovative business model.[34]

For this special occasion, a new collection of 100 pieces – each one-of-a-kind – has been created by designer Frédéric Zavvy at prices ranging from €40,000 to €7 million. Some private commission will be undertaken for clients and, although the focus is on the contemporary, the company does not exclude *a priori* introducing new version of the highly celebrated eggs. The great-granddaughter of the founder, Tatiana Fabergé, was also involved as advisor on the family heritage.[35]

The model proposed by Fabergé may also overcome disadvantages of the normal online shopping sites, that is to say the lack of exclusivity and loss of control. In fact, Fabergé's prospects do not have self-service access to the whole collection but the collections are progressively revealed as the client relationship develops. This kind of interaction allows the brand to have the control of the relationship with the clients: just as customers ring the bell of a boutique, to access Fabergé service, they have to provide phone details so that the advisors can call them back and assist them. Prospects are initially presented with a limited view of the collection, the so-called 'public space', and they gradually explore new pieces by invitation following a dialogue with a Fabergé sales advisor who tailors a selection according to the client's tastes and preferences. Pieces are initially brought by the advisor in a space called the 'Cloud' where the prospect can admire them as they are presented at various distances and various levels of focus to create temptation and aspiration. The following step is to bring the selected pieces to the 'Desk' which is quite similar to that of the traditional boutique and that allows an even closer look at the product.[36]

Jewelry is undoubtedly one of the categories of luxury goods which fits most with this innovative business model because its products can be described with metrics – carats of diamonds, weight of the gold – and they do not require special assistance and human presence such as in the case of ultra-complicated watches; nonetheless Fabergé represents a major breakthrough and reference point for the ultra-luxury brands which wish to take full advantage of the latest technology.

5.4.3 Commercial policies in luxury retailing

The different distribution formats that have been presented in the previous sections clearly show how luxury businesses strive for a balance between exclusivity and accessibility; the former granting prestige; the latter, revenues and economies of scale. Proof of this strategy is the flagship store – the most exclusive – which does not necessarily have to be profitable as long as it strengthens the image of the brand.

In the same way, commercial policies have to seek a trade-off between recreating distance with the client and maximizing profits, the former obtained through high prices, no discounts and limited quantities, whereas the latter is obtained through stock clearance that is almost always accompanied by consistent reductions.

The most common commercial policies in the luxury industry are:

- *Custom made*: products that are made for a specific client and that increase the attributes of exclusivity and handmade
- *Scarcity*: creation, for specific product that is requested by the market, of an offer that is intentionally lower than the demand
- *Limited editions*: special series that is sold for a limited time frame or in limited quantities. Generally featured by low production costs yet high returns in terms of profits and image.
- *Sales*: organized by the manufacturers concurrently at the end of every season and mainly present in the fashion industry

- *Private sales*: organized for closed and small groups of clients, they can feature either pre-season collections at full price or pre-season sales
- *Outlet*.

With the exception of private sales, which are held in private locations and are by invitation only, it can be noted that there is a correlation between formats and individual policies, that is to say they tend to match in terms of degree of exclusivity/accessibility.

Under a theoretical perspective, the same approach could be used for online policies (outlets and sales, for instance, are present in both worlds), but the Internet is an open platform where the information can flow more quickly and widely, and is therefore more difficult to control.

This comes into force particularly when approaching online discounting because although on the one hand brands can control their direct channel by applying the same level of discretion online, they are used in offline sales (highly recommendable indeed); on the other hand, it is more difficult to manage the pure e-discounters than their offline counterparts.

Given the vital importance of the issue, and the potential drawbacks that sample sale websites can have on the brand image, luxury players should absolutely not ignore their presence yet find a way to cope together as the only viable solution to grant the brand the maximum coherence possible in terms of price policies.

5.5 THE IMPORTANCE OF THE HUMAN FACTOR IN LUXURY RETAILING

One of the most common mottoes used by brands in the luxury industry is that they 'Sell dreams rather than products', the symbolic desire being a very powerful element driving the aspirational purchase. Unfortunately, breaking this dream and waking clients up can be very easy if any one of the steps of the long chain that goes from the design to the shop delivery fails. A company can execute all the operations perfectly, create the perfect product, amuse people with a stunning communication, but waste all this effort with the incorrect behavior of a sales advisor. In addition to that, the people working in a boutique are the image, the values and the style of the brand they represent, so they have a responsibility that is just too important to be left to chance and improvization. When customers visit a shop, they in fact expect the experience and emotions promised by the brand in its communications. A successful sales advisor should be characterized by a passion for the sector in which he/she operates and a love of social relations; the first helping the advisor to stay continually up to date and to show expertise, the second to engage the clients and convince them to make the purchase; an effective and complete training is complementary and it should include not only the knowledge of products, materials, technology and manufacturing techniques but also the more difficult to teach 'soft' aspects such as interpersonal skills and behavioral attitudes.

The following sections will present recommendations about how to make the client's dreams come true.

5.5.1 Assisting the client throughout the purchase act

Time is by definition part of the purchase process of a luxury good. The dream is generated in the prospects' mind by gradually discovering the object of desire, time spent gathering information, browsing, deciding and finally waiting for the product. If effectively managed, this wait can be turned not only into an enjoyable moment but also into an opportunity to increase the desire of the customers. Every aspect of the pre, during and after purchase must be carefully managed. Due to its specificities, client relationship management is one of the most difficult subjects to teach because it is almost impossible to write down a formal set of rules and guidelines. As advanced soft skills are required, role-playing and simulation have proved to be the most effective training techniques.

- **The pre-purchase**
  A warm welcome is both a duty of the boutique staff and one of the most powerful tools for generating sales; the popular saying 'there is never a second chance of leaving a good first impression' applies in this case. Very often, unsatisfied clients leave the shop

before even making a purchase. Here are three rules thumb sales advisors should always employ:

- *Treat the client as a king*: When entering a luxury boutique, the client expects to buy the best of the best and accordingly to be considered the most important client in the world. Buying the best of the best means also being the protagonist, the most beautiful and admired in the world. The advisor should assist the customer with utmost attention in this journey to avoid breaking this dream.[37]
- *Be professional yet charming and never aggressive*: A sincere and spontaneous smile should always accompany the visit of a client who must feel comfortable in order to make the purchase. Information should be provided with professionalism and style, but being at the client's disposal means also showing sensitivity in understanding when a warmer attitude or sense of humor is required while remaining respectful but not distant. It is a very delicate balance to be found but very much appreciated by high-net-worth individuals.[38]
- *Never pre-judge or judge the client*: Positive thinking should be the prerogative of every advisor – curiosity in knowing and understanding, rather than labeling the client. The wrong attitude may prove to be very expensive for a luxury brand and lead to a potential loss of sales. Judging a client by the style of dress, or even worse, deciding a priori if his or her identity matches that of a specific brand (brand hyper-identification) is harmful. In addition to creating a sense of discomfort (an obviously negative condition for a purchase), it is absolutely impossible in these postmodern, globalized times to correctly interpret dress codes of people coming from different lifestyles, countries and experiences without being misled.[39]

- **The purchase**
The luxury client has often a good knowledge of the product, at least equal, if not superior to that of the staff. It goes without saying that every employee should know all the products and their specifications in terms of design, manufacturing techniques and materials; and in this sense, the more the sales staff knows, the better. Passion plays an important role in motivating salespeople to stay up to date, especially in the digitalized era where there is

an infinity of sources of information which clients have access to, not to mention the user-generated content. It is positive to make the customer feel like an expert and show off his/her knowledge but it is recommendable, on the other hand, not to be caught unprepared on a specific topic.

One area where sales staff should demonstrate excellence is that of brand knowledge. Every employee must be an ambassador, fan and spokesperson of the brand, its essence and values so that the client – not the advisor – can freely decide whether the universe of the proposed brand fits him/her or not.

When it comes to decision-making, empathy is the most important skill to guide clients to understand their motivations and discover their desires. Sales advisors should therefore be proactive in proposing the items that are likely to match clients' tastes, in listening (verbal) and observing (non-verbal) to refine the choice up to the final decision. Active listening also prevents the staff from presenting either too many options (confusing the client) or those the advisor likes more (misleading the client).

■ **The after-purchase**
Thinking that the mission is completed once the payment has been processed would be a huge mistake. As luxury goods are non-necessary (superfluous) products by definition, it is mandatory to reassure clients that they deserve to reward themselves with the object of their dream and that their expensive purchase was the perfect one in terms of product and brand universe (values, heritage, culture). The relationship must be nurtured both in the short term – by accompanying the client to the exit door, and with a feedback call shortly after the purchase – and in the long term, with invitation to events and product presentations – so that full advantage of any available opportunity for inciting the client return is taken. Under this perspective, even complaints should be considered as opportunities for strengthening the relationship with the customer, because on average, when faced with a problem, clients rarely have a high expectation that it will be solved. The most common attitude is to change shop or brand and possibly mitigate the frustration through negative word of mouth among their peers rather than raising the issue.

It goes without saying that a well-addressed problem can convert an unsatisfied client into the most loyal fan of the brand

and, what's more, these rare opportunities of hearing the client are free of charge.

Uncontrolled messages have to be avoided as much as possible, especially in the web 2.0 era where buzzes can travel very fast around the world, so it is compulsory to actively listen and understand the problem, reassure that corrective action will be taken and keep the client informed about how the solution is proceeding.

5.5.2 The boutique manager

A luxury brand is a universe of emotions and promises that clients expect to be satisfied when entering a store to purchase a product. As previously seen, the right training is a fundamental part of the induction of a new salesperson, nonetheless the store manager is the supreme guardian of this promise having to effectively manage each member of the team so that the final result is met. Due to the importance of the role, and due to the direct contact with the final customer, a store manager of a retail group or brand very often has direct access to the CEO, and it is no surprise that talented managers are very rare to find and consequently the object of fierce competition among companies.

In addition to the skills of a good sales advisor, a boutique manager must possess a broad spectrum of knowledge comprising[40]:

■ Leadership abilities, to build a team that is always on the ball, that is to say, strong, consistent and motivated to continuously learning
■ Technical knowledge, especially in complex products such as fine cars and timepieces
■ Managerial skills, a store being like a subsidiary company with daily issues like purchasing, managing stocks, managing human resources and handling sales and promotional budgets
■ Marketing, public relations and communication abilities, by attending social events and keeping a pulse on the local market,

especially in the case of multibrand boutiques where making the right purchase is the key to satisfying client tastes and needs.

5.5.3   The importance of the human factor in luxury e-retailing

Like its brick and mortar counterpart, an online boutique must be considered a touchpoint with the client as well as a manifestation of the brand identity.

Although the interaction is virtual, rather than physical, the dream still has to be created and nurtured, and the client should still be accompanied throughout the purchase act. E-retailing has specific requirements, some of which are also opportunities for enhancing the brand experience and generation of revenue.

- **The pre-purchase**: Thanks to digital technologies – identification and e-CRM functionalities in particular – a broader array of information about the connected client (shopping histories, habits and preferences) are easily retrievable and instantly available, so that the service is better customized and the customer can be properly welcomed in the store.
- **The purchase**: When requiring assistance, e-luxury clients have to be instantaneously followed up by a sales advisor using different modalities such as phone, e-mail, chat, call-back options. Response speed is even more important than offline, and this service must be provided in several languages, 24 hours a day, 7 days a week, 365 days a year. The virtual boutique is expected to be continually open and the brand and product knowledge continually available. Anytime is good for creating the dream in the consumer. Internet is sometimes considered the world of instantaneous, but the client can enjoy the wait in the same way he or she does offline, especially when it comes to delivery time, which is not necessarily shorter than offline. While being difficult to replicate the same customer experience of the offline store online, functionalities like instant video chatting may help those more traditional clients who are seeking opinions and suggestions from an educated source.[41]

■ **The after purchase**: Any opportunity for making the client come back must be leveraged. In addition to constant communication about novelties, initiatives and events, effective online client management can be supported by personalized communication and marketing initiatives leading to fidelity and purchase reiteration. E-mail offers, in particular, are the online equivalent of cross- and up-selling opportunities that in-store sales associates master by giving recommendations on how to combine different products or to match a specific item with complementary ones.[42]

In conclusion, it can be affirmed that Internet is increasingly becoming a complementary tool to the traditional activities of the luxury businesses.

CASE STUDY 5.5A: ADAPTING TO TIMES; NEW LUXE AND NEW CLIENTS ACCORDING TO THE FOUNDATION DE LA HAUTE HORLOGERIE (INTERVIEW)

The process of democratization experienced by the luxury sector at the end of twentieth century brought many changes in the way brands approach consumers. The big players of the industry have changed their philosophy and are not looking for a rare public but for the rarity that is in all of us; not an elite, but the elitism that is in each of us. According to the French philosopher Gilles Lipovetsky,[43] the purchase of an expensive luxury object 20 years ago was proof of wealth and belonging to a particular social class, whereas today it represents an expression of who we are, our tastes, our relation with the arts, our esthetic aspirations and our cultural identity. Luxury objects tell the history of their clients, in a logic that is cultural rather than statutory. This change has implied a shift in needs and expectations at the time consumers purchase a luxury good. 'In a time frame encompassing slightly more than a generation, the watch has changed its function, moving from timekeeping device to social symbol and – following the democratization process of luxury brands – from social to cultural symbol', says Mr. Gianfranco Ritschel, delegate of the Fondation de La Haute Horlogerie and major retail expert and trainer in the watch industry. 'The sales of a high-end watch today', he continues, 'is very similar to that of a piece of art. In our training courses at FHH we suggest building the discourse with the client in four stages:

1. The brand and its world: heritage, history, anecdotes, golden times, iconic products
2. Esthetics of the brand: *raison d'etre*, style, design principles, lines, proportions and so on
3. Product details, finishing, executions
4. Manufacturing techniques, materials, functions and mechanism complications.

It is only by respecting this chronology that it is possible to create a presentation that goes beyond the mere product description. Interest and tension are progressive and the client won't decide simply whether or not to buy, but he will recognize greater value in the product.' During the interview, Mr. Ritschel also agrees with the need to guide the client toward personal self-expression. 'In our modern selling techniques, we teach our trainees to begin with a discovery phase of the client. Salespeople have to understand first the true motivations of the prospect and build a customized presentation accordingly.' Regarding the information power shift, he underlines the increasing complexity of the sales work: 'Knowing everything about the brand is key, but today it is not enough just to explain the difference between products of two different brands, the client wants to know why these differences exist. Advertising and press releases show by the same token, an increasing level of technical information, witnessing the will of renowned houses to feature their profile as highly horological. This becomes for salespeople a further challenge to cope with, and the increasingly broad range of information available on the Internet doesn't help either.' When it comes to recommendations, Mr. Ritschel concludes: 'Given the increasing complexity of this work, personnel training cannot be left exclusively to up the boutique director who, even if skillful and capable, would simply not have the time to do it. At FHH, in addition to providing specific courses, we recommend creating a self-learning boutique, and environment in which, thanks to specific educational and management tools, personal development becomes an attitude. To respond to these needs, we have also created a dedicated device, called the Watch@Tablet®.'

CASE STUDY 5.5B: THE WATCH@TABLET®

At a time when ultra-complicated watches are becoming more and more popular and brands are proposing a multitude of models, the risk of being unable to reply accurately and instantly to a question about a specific function or model is very high. Added to that, connoisseurs are used to spending their spare time navigating forums, blogs and any kind of watch-related websites, it goes without saying that in order to manage all the information of the web 2.0 era, traditional training tools are no longer enough. Aficionados, on the other hand, who are prepared to invest a considerable sum in their watch, certainly want to be reassured they have made the right choice and do not wish to have to seek advice somewhere else. To address this specific need, the Fondation de la Haute Horlogerie (FHH) has developed a touch screen notebook – the **Watch@Tablet®** – which serves as training tool, but which can be also called on as a selling aid to show customers specific aspects of fine watchmaking that would otherwise be too complex to describe, for example, features of the manufacturing process, a particular *métier d'art* or a function found only on exceptional timepieces. All the content – fully interactive via touch screen and illustrated throughout with informative animations – has been designed and developed for the sales needs: not extremely technical, not too scientific nor too broad, yet complete and much more didactical than an Internet search, thanks to the contribution of experts in the fields of retail, watchmaking, gemology and history.

Watch@Tablet® is divided into three zones. The first is reserved for the 29 partner-brands of the FHH, with pages and animations to present each one. The second is devoted to essential information on watchmaking and gemology as a complement to the sales associates' own valuable knowledge, for example how a mechanical watch functions, how to serve, repair and maintain a watch, the illustrated explanations of 20 complications, a glossary with 250 words explained through text, animations and illustrations. It also includes a 'News' area, thanks to which staff can regularly receive updates sent by an FHH journalist about new models or events without leaving their place of work.

The third section contains information for the retailer (including training modules proposed by the FHH and a training book with quizzes, questionnaires and other activities) plus a reserved space, which can include the brands' own working documents, developed exclusively for sales associates in their distribution networks.

Thanks to this tablet, customers will enjoy discovering countless fascinating aspects of fine watchmaking in an intelligent and documented way.

6

INTERNET, SOCIAL MEDIA AND LUXURY STRATEGY

Fleur Gastaldi

6.1 INTRODUCTION

Over the past decade, a brand new mass medium has made a dramatic appearance in the form of the Internet – with its major application, the World Wide Web, commonly known as the web. The Internet has drastically changed all traditional business models. In the luxury industry, there has been fierce questioning about how to approach this growing phenomenon, and how to preserve a unique brand image in the open world offered by the Internet. Luxury brands have long debated how to integrate this powerful and intrusive channel of mass communication into the intimacy of an exclusive luxury brand's strategy.

Massively penetrating households in the early 2000s in the United States and in the mid-2000s in Europe, the web quickly became a very personal communication channel in an expanding virtual distribution place. Since, the luxury industry has had to rethink how to drive its business basics in order to keep up with consumers' changing behaviors and expectations. Simply being unique would no longer be enough to survive in the market.

The Internet has today reached a level of stability, and luxury businesses should be ready to plunge into the World Wide (or should we say *wild*) Web. While it symbolizes a huge technological step for humankind, the Internet has also introduced a complete cultural shift on the worldwide consumer market.

The temptation is to just throw a brand out into the jungle – that is, the web. However, the stakes and costs are high, especially in the luxury industry. The competitive advantage generated by the web would only qualify as successful for those who treat the web with brand intelligence, strategic skill and business vision. In the end, what is of value for the offline market also applies to the online market.

6.2 DEFINING A WEB STRATEGY IS GOOD; ENVISIONING AN INTEGRATED STRATEGY IS BETTER

How to get on to the web and how to get the web into your strategy?

Luxury is for the happy few. The Internet is wide open to anyone. What could have initially been perceived as a dead-end situation is not any more. Today the web offers a qualitative medium along with many meaningful marketing opportunities. Moreover, since the late 2000s, the web seems to have reached a stage of refinement offering highly creative designs, efficient functionalities and trustworthy secured transaction systems.

All businesses are now aware that a dedicated website is not sufficient in itself to achieve a successful e-marketing strategy. In 2010, about 92 percent of web users used a search engine to reach the brand websites they wanted to access.[1] Thus, it is becoming compulsory for a branded website to rank first on any related brand web search. And that is a basic, at least it should be . . . A brand with a historically strong identity risks losing some of its strength in the eye of the customer if it does not appear among the first results in any brand-associated web search.

6.2.1 Developing the right web marketing approach

a. e-Branding and luxury

Web marketing is all about getting a brand out there and developing brand visibility combined with positive brand exposure. Search engines are the first tools to focus on: this is called 'search engine optimization' or SEO. When dealing with search engines, the main ones should be targeted per market: Google, Yahoo and Bing for most Western countries; Baidu for China; Yandex for Russia. The

SEO uses the legitimacy a brand naturally possesses as a basis to rank first on branded searches. Creating content related to all the brand's characteristics, registering brand names and web domains, subscribing to the main industry directories, developing web partnerships with targeted online media and distributors are all keys to achieving the right SEO for the brand.

A further step is to include all associated topics: a branded website should be able to rank well on all its industry's related searches. These can be as diverse as 'Easter package hotel and spa', 'Jewerly for Christmas', 'designer winter coat' or 'women silk cheich scarf'. The whole purpose of visibility on the web is to secure web traffic that is expanding. Since higher traffic means an increased volume of web visitors, it can be inferred than the whole business will be positively impacted. Brands should regard the web as a business multiplier: web visitors may wish to visit their boutiques or prefer to purchase online.

Knowing the audience is key to a web marketing strategy. The behavior of a web user will depend on specific profiles, whether the user is a traditional offline customer, a returning visitor, a demanding loyal client or an Internet-savvy new customer. User categories should then be defined: former brand customers, current brand addicts, potential customers, curious web visitors or random shopping addicts. Some will visit a website before buying in a physical boutique; some will prefer the price guarantee of a well-known online retailer instead of shopping on the brand e-shop directly. An integrated web marketing strategy should aim to ensure that no cannibalization could damage any of the brand's cherished distribution channels.

The very first tool of a web marketing strategy remains the brand's website. An efficient web user experience is obtained when the right balance between esthetics and usability is reached. In one click, any web user should be able to access the main functionalities: an online shop, a contact form or an e-newsletter registration form. The right layout and a clear site menu will increase user acceptance of the brand website and hopefully overall user satisfaction. Four aspects of a brand website should be the core focus: navigation and usability, value of the content, home page (users spend no more than ten seconds on a page), and guarantee of privacy and security (Figure 6.1).

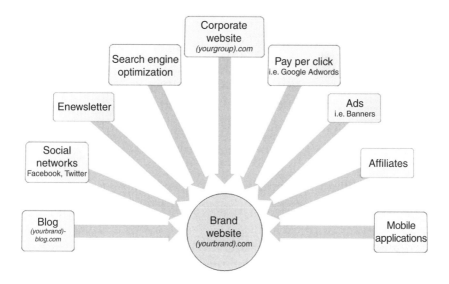

FIGURE 6.1 **Sources of website traffic and revenue**

b. Recreating the experience

Luxury products or services mean high prices. Thus, e-customers expect to receive an experience in return. An attractive website using flash animation will soon disappoint if found to be incomplete or inefficient. Today's luxury consumer tends to be more and more Internet-savvy and extremely demanding toward online services. A branded website should be thought of as an implicit contract between the brand and the web user. The information published on any branded website should be accurate, up-to-date and worth the visit. Details and images should reflect both the brand's image and the reality of its products. Any luxury brand should reach an ideal balance between attractive animation and visuals, combined with easy navigation.

The brand's website is the central marketing tool to create an emotional relationship with potential customers. It offers a high level of services such as brand information, exclusive news and goodies. The website is just the front window display of the brand, on which many functionalities can be added, such as virtual fitting rooms, interactive size guides, virtual showrooms, virtual customer service hosts and suggestions to match items and tools to recreate specific looks. Any website should also feature an up-to-date offline boutique locator which can be a simple list of shops or an elaborate mobile geolocation application which will locate the closest boutique.

Web marketing is about maintaining the right balance between the resources spent in attracting visitors to the website and developing a complete online offer. As in traditional marketing, a web visitor will only become valuable once the brand affinity is realized.

c. The question of e-commerce

The web is a mass medium that contrasts completely with the traditional codes of exclusivity associated with the luxury industry, and has long been simply rejected by the luxury industry for being an illegitimate distribution channel. Even now, some major luxury brands remain reluctant to open an e-commerce platform. Early 2011, the well-recognized couture brand Chanel runs a branded website with no e-commerce platform (except for one US cosmetic website). In contrast, the luxury PPR Group decided to develop e-commerce platforms for all its brands. Between these two positions, Dior seems to prefer web exposure to e-commerce implication. Indeed, a Dior brand search on Google.com features various websites such as dior.com, ladydior.com, diorjoillerie.com, diorcouture.com, diorhomme.com, while the brand still offers a very limited product range available for online purchase.

An e-commerce strategy does not only mean accepting to manage an e-boutique, it also implies maintaining an online catalog and reorganizing the logistics with complex stock issues across the multiple channels. This represents a real change for any business.

Of course, the web can be an uncontrolled channel of communication and distribution and may present a high risk of counterfeiting and brand use abuse. Within the luxury industry, fashion and cosmetics are well ahead in terms of e-commerce compared to the watch and jewelry branches, which present a traditional distribution system that is key in explaining this situation.[2]

Another explanation for this reluctance to adopt an e-commerce strategy lies in the issue of price display. An e-commerce strategy means that a brand business has to globally rethink its distribution

FLEUR GASTALDI

but also to accept making prices public. The year 2010 marked a tremendous change globally in the luxury industry's approach to the web. After two years of deep economic crisis, the web appeared as an economic opportunity for all businesses, particularly regarding the success of price comparison websites and the trend for a more discreet consumer behavior.

CASE STUDY 1: THE ORIENT-EXPRESS GROUP

Using web marketing to maintain a competitive share on the luxury travel market

Since 1982, the Orient-Express group has been the proud owner of the legendary Venice Simplon-Orient-Express (VSOE) train, along with other luxury trains, cruises and hotels. The UK-based hospitality and travel group is a middle-size company in a very competitive environment. A journey aboard the VSOE costs from €1860 for the traditional Paris to Venice route, to €6580 for the historical 1883 Paris to Istanbul journey. The VSOE train is a landmark in the history of transportation . . . with no shower on board. Nonetheless, clients do purchase their journeys online on the website www.orient-express.com.

The Orient-Express group is a good example of a company that has understood the shift in its customers' wishes. During the early 2000s, the company focused on implementing a web marketing team which would efficiently develop the practice of Search Engine Optimization, combined with a great concern for website usability and look. The website of the Orient-Express has undergone three redesigns in the last seven years. The group has developed a Content Management System in order to enable all hotel and train offers and content to be anticipated and updated internally; it has put in place an affiliation program and has been working on developing dynamic packaging along with hotel and train bookings. Lately, the Orient-Express train has opened Facebook and Twitter accounts. Today Orient-Express sells train journeys, cruises trips and hotel packages in 25 countries, across five continents. Orient-Express runs more than 50 websites internally, including its corporate website, intranet and extranet, as well as the website of each individual property.[3]

6.2.2 The e-Marketing mix: Place, product, price, promotion

As for offline marketing, a thorough study of the e-marketing mix is essential. Only a well-balanced e-marketing mix can be efficient on the online market. The basics are alike: the product has to be attractive; the price competitive; the promotion efficient; and the distribution consistent and secured. The specificity of the luxury industry lies in the fact that brand image is fragile and the level of tolerance of luxury brand addicts is low.

Luxury businesses should also revisit the traditional codes of the luxury industry when applied to the web. Understanding the web users' new behaviors and expectations and integrating the online into the global brand strategy are key aspects.

a. The web customer's scanning behavior (product and pricing)

A brand choosing to start a web strategy should commit itself wholeheartedly. A consumer might quickly forget about his visit to a new e-commerce website if the product range is too poor. The brand should therefore offer a substantial product range including some of the brand's newest product lines, on which the brand's latest communication is based. The web has to reflect the life of the brand in any case.

As for the offline market, buying a luxury product is a purchasing act which also implies an emotional investment in the brand. The online purchase is a complete process: atmosphere, product description, shipping options, product guarantee and after-sales customer services. All these aspects of the purchasing process have to be highly qualitative, as trust will only be achieved if the satisfaction of the client remains intact.

In the online world, the customer is alone in front of a computer screen before making a purchase. The e-customer searches and compares freely. On the web, prices are widely displayed. No boutique doors to put random visitors off and no place to hide. These aspects make it clear that on the web a luxury product should never be associated only with a price; instead, a product should always be associated with a brand's unique quality of service, an exceptional online customer service, a product guarantee, an included follow-up on order, an exchange or refund facility, an express and secured delivery, a product personalization service or a discreet delivery option. All added-value will directly be legitimating any price in the eye of the online customer.

Moreover, displaying prices widely also raises the question of price parity. When everyone has access to the prices of a luxury hotel room or a designer diamond ring, the different distribution channels then become direct competitors on the web. A brand can no longer offer exceptional prices on its own brand website without granting special compensating rates or a different packaged offer to the rest of its distribution partners. The best example of this is in the luxury hospitality industry. A five-star luxury hotel will practice yield management over its room prices, opening/closing special rates according to its occupancy forecast. However, hotels contract with online travel agents such as Expedia, with such obligation as to guarantee a 20 percent lower rate over some room rates. The hotel then adapts its special offer rates according to this restriction. Now, a client from a traditional travel agency buys a package with a stay in this hotel plus other options, at a packaged price. The client sees a special offer on Expedia and then discovers the room rate is lower than the one his travel agent got him for a standard room. The whole industry is currently rethinking how it contracts with online and offline travel agents and other e-distribution partners. Product pricing is therefore becoming much more complicated and rules have to change.

An elaborated e-pricing strategy should always be built in order to avoid cannibalizing any distribution channel. Considering that the prices are displayed widely, inconsistent public pricing also risks damaging the customer's opinion of the brand image.

b. Dealing with traditional distribution actors (place)

France is historically one of the main producers of luxury goods. According to the Benchmark Group, 85 percent of French Internet users would visit a luxury brand website before visiting a boutique for a purchase.[4]

When placing a brand on the online market, it is essential to understand that a website represents a unique channel for building a strong relationship with consumers, and surely the one channel a brand shouldn't miss out on. However, brands are also being pressurized by traditional offline partners who want to keep their diminishing market share, even though consumers don't understand it this way. A brand should legitimately develop its own web strategy and at the same time consider partnering with other recognized online players and strategically supporting its offline purchasing points. Many options are available to the businesses, including web opportunities such as developing a specific website to help partners to sell better: a dedicated extranet. Too often forgotten, the extranet can be a great tool to gather all distribution partners into the brand global strategy, giving them the marketing tools to sell better; such as information about the brand's latest products, product guides, a space to send feedback to the brand and so on.

Another issue in placing a brand and its products on the online place concerns price comparison websites. Cheap, mass-market vulgar. Maybe. However, rethinking the web as a pleasant place to be, why wouldn't luxury brands accept to be featured next to each other . . . as they are on the fancy boulevards? It is all a question of qualitative content.

c. Promotion and communication

With the success of the Internet, web advertising is booming. The main promotion tools on the web are pay-per-click ads on search engines and third-party websites, promotional banners and affiliation programs. The approach to web advertising so far has been wild. But today, regulation is enforcing the set of rules. All brands have to make sure their name does not suffer from any abuse, as preserving a brand name also means reserving a legitimate promotional space. Despite these abuses, web advertising offers a great level of targeting possibilities: by location, by city, by area, by medium and so on. This refined targeting possibility enables all brands to be part of the web advertising in accordance with their marketing budgets.

A website's global performance in terms of traffic and returning visitors impacts the sales of the whole business. On the online market, a brand may choose to offer either similar or distinct products or services compared to those available in boutiques and agencies. With the aim of avoiding cannibalization among its own distribution schema, a brand may select different added-value options dedicated to its online-sold products: specific packaging and services to boost the average purchase, secured delivery options and unique loyalty programs. Anyhow, the added-value a website offers to its visitors and customers will also evolve along with the new standards of web marketing.

6.3 TAKING WEB STRATEGY TO NEW CHALLENGES

Today's expectation toward qualitative online information and safe e-commerce services is increasingly high. And luxury clients are no exception to the rule. A website is today the brand's shop window, as well as being a service offered to all visitors. Personalizing the web experience therefore becomes a leading success factor.

As competition is more and more innovative, options to stand out on the web are wide. Still, issues of logistics have to be addressed. The promise of a customer experience should not be damaged by a lack of service. We are talking about luxury. We are talking about a qualitative web. Here is the real challenge.

6.3.1 Optimizing existing assets and developing new ones

Internet is evolving at a tremendous pace. So are its players. And businesses are trying to keep up. Optimizing the existing company's resources is an essential first step for all businesses, while adapting to the e-market's new forces should never be under-evaluated.

With such a fast pace of innovation, brands can get a huge competitive advantage by keeping informed and sharing information about Internet strategies with all stakeholders such as business partners, competitors and customers. Resources are plenty, but businesses have to see and understand them.

a. Anticipation and vision

On the online market, businesses should aim to have a clear understanding of their environment in order to position brands accordingly. Most businesses try to learn from web best practices and understand these ongoing changes. In such a flourishing environment, any business can be successful with a bit of anticipation and vision. This can be internally managed by recruiting relevant profiles or by participating in online forums, or in congresses, or finally by simply endorsing the role of an Internet user exploring what the web has to offer.

One of the advantages of web marketing is the availability of immediate metrics. Key indicators should point the brand's marketing actions in the right direction. With Google's (contested) leadership, all businesses can now access useful, zero-cost information: their own. The web-based Google Analytics platform is one of the best applications from Google. With such a tremendous leadership of one big actor, all other competitors are trying to compete by offering free statistics tools and other applications. This is a great asset for all businesses to enter the online market.

Following a business's website performances is the best data for understanding customers and what they are looking for, as well as how, but also where they are coming from and going to. With such immediate data available, any marketing action turns out to be traceable within minutes. How satisfying it is in such a virtual world to be able to obtain tangible results of any marketing campaign undertaken.

In this quest for understanding and anticipating in the online market, many other web actors can be considered. Qualitative web chats and forums and specialized blogs are also wonderful sources of information and ideas for any web marketers. With the emergence of the Internet, a lot of valuable information has become accessible to all, giving substantial clues to all type of businesses entering the online market.

b. Developing a substantial competitive advantage

A web strategy should be thought out carefully and many objectives addressed: developing a database using newsletter co-registration with partners, targeting another type of consumer by promoting a mobile phone application, creating the buzz with targeted web-pure players in a win-win partnership and so on. Many e-marketing opportunities are to be explored; however, a brand should always remember to remain close to its audience, as customers will be its very first ambassadors.

Customizing the experience of any luxury brand customer is key. Reproducing a luxury brand experience on a website is a priority. Personalization is about inviting the simple web visitor to a better place. This can be a virtual private space where visitors can find a customized welcoming message, their own preferences saved for later visits or any suggestions of relevant products and services according to the place of residence, latest purchases and interests. Private access to a website is a marvelous opportunity for a brand to segment the information sent and build an exclusive relationship to share confidential news, limited virtual invitations to privileged video show presentations or special birthday invitations to visit the closest boutique. Customizing the experience is an effective gateway to measure the audience value and push further brand segmentation.

c. e-CRM as knowing customers and acquiring new ones

A web visitor is far more volatile than the customer of a physical boutique. To develop customer loyalty, luxury businesses need to build unique relationships with their web audience. A right balance between rationality and emotionality is key to creating a strong link, while a positive user experience will ensure a repeat visit in the near future.

E-mail communication is a good web marketing tool to build strong relationships. A brand should approach e-mailing as a long-term process of expanding customer loyalty and not solely as an immediate push for purchase. Disappointment might be big for the brand... and for the customer. Four essential components should be considered when planning an e-mailing campaign: name of the sender as a the seal of authenticity; teasing object to guarantee a better opening rate; substantial content elaborated by selecting two or three maximum calls of action (register to the private space, visit the new collection, become a fan on Facebook); and, of course, all the legal privacy aspects of e-mailing such as profile preferences and unsubscribe option.

CASE STUDY 2: BOUCHERON

When luxury jewelry manages anticipation combined with e-commerce strategy

When most exclusive luxury brands remained skeptical about how to approach the web as a strategy, Boucheron was one of the first brands in Europe to throw itself into the web world, opening its first e-boutique in September 2007. Boucheron's General Director, J.C. Bédos, admits that the brand initially went in blind without any idea about the potential business development it would incur. Boucheron focused on the e-services the brand should offer on the Internet with the aim of selling quality to its prospects. In one year the website registered a 400 percent increase in audience figures. Boucheron chose not to rest on such positive results and in 2008, to coincide with the celebration of its 150th anniversary, the brand launched a new improved website adopting a sophisticated graphic chart, and redesigning its website usability based on client feedback. Product and service descriptions became clearer and more accurate. Boucheron soon realized that the web strategy had brought new types of clients, clients they would never have attracted in a traditional and exclusive boutique. Boucheron.com soon became a complementary distribution channel, complementary to traditional offline shops, not a competitor.[5]

In 2008, when the 'Quatre' ring collection was released in shops and widely advertised in the chic arrondissements of Paris, the whole collection became available almost simultaneously online. When navigating the Boucheron.com website, two key aspects stand out: the website is simple and the visuals are of a very high quality. Boucheron.com offers product personalization options, a size guide and in November 2010 the jewelry brand introduced myboucheron.com, a virtual space offering the customer a virtual experience of the products with the possibility to try a ring or a watch on virtually, from the comfort of the customer's home.

6.3.2 Dealing with increasing interaction from web audience

New technologies are emerging at a faster pace than companies can swallow[6]

The Internet economy is entering a stage of maturity: content is more qualitative, legal frames are being implemented and businesses, along with users, now have a better understanding of the media. A brand publishes some content, and this content is duplicated on a blog, whose audience will soon relay it on the pages of Facebook. The web 2.0 is all about information sharing. The information is shared by referrers to receivers, who become in turn referrers.

It is understood that most businesses should not aim to handle all the latest technologies and media, as investments are high and the return on investment can be tricky. However, all should agree that they need to understand the most popular ones according to their own market.

a. Interacting and social networking

The web 2.0 is all about sending the relevant message to an interconnected network of users. No brand can ignore this interaction and social networks are becoming so powerful that they are becoming a tricky issue for the next generation of web marketing. While all businesses are aware that social networks represent a costless step to take, few manage to handle such networks as they would like.

Clearly, businesses are still figuring out how to optimize social networks efficiently and turn them into a sustainable means of communication. For luxury brands, it is another huge challenge to decide how to combine their cherished exclusivity to this major shift in communication. Facebook, the leading network, overtook Google.com's US audience for the first time in March 2010, with a superior weekly volume of visits.[7] Highly symbolic. From 'searchable', the Internet is now becoming 'sociable':

> Microsoft made computers easy for everyone to use. Google helps us search out data. YouTube keeps us entertained. But Facebook has a huge advantage over those other sites: the emotional investment of its users.[8]

Social media imply a very high degree of emotional and personal reaction. Consistent marketing skills are needed to approach social media optimization (SMO), especially as the pace of these networks is so fast. No rules are yet enforced as the long-term impact of such marketing tools has not yet been measured due to a lack of experience and time. The question is open as to which approach luxury businesses will choose to handle the exclusivity of their brand when using such mass media. But undeniably, no brand can ignore social media today. In early 2004, the Facebook adventure started in a dorm room of Harvard. Before the end of the year, the social network had already registered 1 million users. Six years later, in 2010, Facebook reached 500 million active users worldwide, 30 percent of whom are in the United States.

> If the website were granted terra firma, it would be the world's third largest country by population, two-thirds bigger than the U.S.[9]

Understanding such powerful social media as Facebook implies more than just adding some novelties on a page or new pictures every couple of days. According to the Facebook data center, an average user is 'friend' with 130 other Facebook users and interacts with 80 community pages, groups and events. Users spend over 700 billion minutes per month on the social media.[10] What is at stake is the establishment of a consistent relationship with the brand's fans. Comprehensive user analysis and an appropriate selection of information to share are essential. Social networks can be feared, but mostly they should be considered as fantastic opportunity to acquire new brand ambassadors.

b. Facing and learning about social media

Social networks are a new global approach to marketing brand information and communicating a unique image. Apart from Facebook, other networks are also active on the web: Twitter is a major channel for shorter information, while blogs are a better opportunity for a brand to develop a more casual tone and provide live feeds, fashion show videos, impromptu celebrity interviews and so on.

The social media are undergoing major changes themselves, noticeably with the arrival of the long-expected mobile market. In 2010, more than 200 million active users accessed Facebook through their mobile devices or smart phones. Mobile users appear to be twice as active on Facebook as non-mobile users.[11] Major evolutions in the way to approach social networks are likely to become the focus in the coming years.

Poor messages and uninteresting information won't make a brand's social network strategy efficient. Once a brand gets on the social networks, it has to play their game. Again, optimization remains a key aspect. When a brand launches a photo contest for Facebook fans, it should post a message, 'status', offering the Facebook fans the possibility to post a photo staging a story with the brand's product. The brand thus creates an interest or maybe a product purchase and definitely a word of mouth effect. Let's go further. The brand announces that the winner will be selected on the basis of the number of 'Like button' clicks the photo will receive. The brand is now pushing the contestants to share their participation with their network of Facebook 'friends', calling them to visit the brand's Facebook page. Finally, since there is an increase in traffic on the brand's Facebook page, the brand can see this peak of traffic as an opportunity to develop its own database by enticing visitors to register to the brand's e-newsletter with a link redirecting to the brand's website.

A social network page is a great opportunity to relay a modern and lively brand image by giving away the latest novelties and organizing contests that will enable fans to be part of the brand experience. On social networks, brands should clearly state what they expect from their 'fans' (Facebook) or their 'followers' (Twitter). The results of the messages are traceable: a brand posts a status and collects many reactions on the Facebook page, for instance, and with a positive status, the number of 'fans' will substantially increase, and so on. Social media allow a new two-way approach with potential customers: the brand talks and the visitor reacts.

This approach contrasts with the approach of an official brand website, as on the social media, the brand talks to its audience. Casual though they may be, social media still require a good social media strategy based on substantial business objectives.

6.4 CONCLUSIONS

Undeniably, the widespread use of the Internet has created an economic environment of fast-moving competitors and partners. Any web-pure player can become a leader overnight while customers can play substantial roles in any brand dealing with social networks. Considering this fast-moving business environment, it has become necessary for luxury brands to address the question of their presence on the web and consider both successful web marketing and e-commerce strategies as two essential business objectives. Luxury brands cannot expand online business if they neglect their web traffic optimization and brand exposure on the web. At the same time, a perfect web marketing strategy is of little use when not combined with a qualitative online-purchasing e-commerce approach.

Together with e-commerce, web marketing should be approached as a sustainable business investment for a brand. Sustainable web marketing cannot be focused on the immediate purchase, but instead should be based on long-term objectives such as driving targeted traffic, offering qualitative content and developing the visitor and customer loyalty. The traditional balance between offline and online channels is obviously changing. However, the whole distribution mix should benefit from an efficient web strategy in the long-term.

Any web and e-commerce strategy is not just about running a website. E-commerce is much more about driving the relevant traffic to a branded and virtual location, whose backstage is made of perfect logistic and stock management. In other words, e-business is simply about business.

This chapter has voluntarily adopted a positive tone. There are, in these tremendous changes, fantastic opportunities for brand marketers to successfully achieve brand goals. This does not imply that the web is without risk. Many aspects are still to be legally framed, such as brand protection and counterfeiting issues, as well as endangered selective distribution. However, considering the balance between the pluses and the minuses, the web remains a positive evolution in the marketing world. And it is certainly never too late to get onto the web strategy. It changes so fast that any brand might just arrive at the right moment to catch the train, using businesses' best practices. Skill and experience are key to the success of a business on the web, and web marketing should be included in any business strategy.

University of Winchester

Customer ID: ****7772

Items that you have borrowed

Title: Luxury strategy in action
ID: 9603861023
Due: 25 November 2020

Total items: 1
Account balance: £2.40
16/11/2020 16:02
Borrowed: 1
Overdue: 0
Hold requests: 0
Ready for collection: 0

7

BRANDING PRINCIPLES IN THE LUXURY INDUSTRY

Tinne Van Gorp

7.1 INTRODUCTION

Over the years, the notion of luxury has changed. In the classical luxury of the eighteenth and nineteenth centuries, the focus was on the product; during the 1920s this focus shifted to the product's creator. In the 1970s, luxury became dominated by the media – images and luxury became the brand.[1] Changing consumer behavior and competition in the luxury market explain the shifting notion of luxury.

An increase in purchasing power due to rising salaries, the emancipation of women and an overall trend of price reductions meant that luxury products were no longer reserved for a minority. It could be said from now on 'Lidl finances Chanel'.[2] Consumers trade down in product categories that are of minor importance to them in order to save sufficient funds to trade up in others. It is not the culture that is important to these consumers, but the price. Cheap clothes are combined with expensive accessories.[3]

In the 1980s, the fashion sector became increasingly competitive because of new entrants, the diversification of existing luxury players into new activities and globalization. This trend was further accelerated by the emergence of luxury conglomerates, which took over small- and medium-sized luxury businesses. These conglomerates have one main brand. For example, PPR owns the brand Gucci.[4]

When purchasing a luxury handbag, customers can choose from among a vast number of brands. The purchase of a luxury handbag is an occasional decision. In environments where competition is fierce, brands become hallmarks. If the scope for differentiation is limited, the emphasis shifts from the product to its image. The core of companies has thus shifted from the production of things to the production of images. Brands have become projects of meaning, and the product has become one of the manifestations of the brand.[5] Further, in the fashion market, products gradually change due to planned obsolescence, but the brand remains more or less constant. Brand building thus gets a prominent role.

This chapter builds on the framework developed by Fionda and Moore.[6] The authors identified the key characteristics of a luxury fashion brand. In this chapter, the results of a case study including the luxury leather goods brands Bottega Veneta, Delvaux, Loewe, Louis Vuitton and Prada will be given.

7.2 APPROACHES TO LUXURY BRAND BUILDING

There are two different approaches to luxury brand building.[7] These approaches resulted from two different business models for luxury brands. The brands that belong to the first business model are those with a long history behind them, while the second business model comprises relatively new brands; those lacking history.

Companies adopting the first business model find their roots mainly in Europe. Their brands put emphasis on the actual product, its craftsmanship, its uniqueness and its rarity as a factor of success. Brands that belong to the first group can be visualized using a pyramid in which three or more different levels interact. At the top of the pyramid one finds the *griffe*, at the second level, the luxury brand, and at the bottom, the upper-range brand. *Griffe* is the height of luxury. The creator's signature is engraved on unique creations. A special order of luxury leather goods, which results in a unique product, is an example of products in this category. This is the equivalent of *Haute Couture* for clothing. The second level contains the luxury brands. These products are manufactured in small series within workshops, Hermès, for example, and emphasize handmade work and craftsmanship. When it comes to clothing, one can find here the ready-to-wear collection. The third level comprises upper-range brands. These brands are made in series, also called streamlined mass production, but have the highest quality within their category. Examples are Dior, Chanel and Yves Saint Laurent cosmetics. In this pyramid model, the base feeds the brand's overall cash flow, while there must be a constant regeneration of value at the top. At this point, creativity, the signature and the creator come in and supply the brand with its artistic inventiveness.[8]

The creator is at the top of the pyramid. The whole system functions around this creator and its name. Going down the pyramid from top to bottom, the level of creativity, the levels of prestige and the levels of price decrease. Prices decrease by going from the top to the bottom but never reach the level of the lowest prices in the category. A lipstick can be sold at only €20 but is still three times more expensive than identical products within its category.[9]

The second business model is adopted mainly by US-based companies that concentrate much more on merchandizing, the atmosphere and image created by their stores. These relatively new brands recognized the importance of the store in creating an atmosphere, in making a genuine impression and in making the values of the brand visible. *What we can see is the creation of a dichotomy between 'history' and the product on the one hand, and 'stories' and distribution on the other.*[10] Besides their flagships and stores, communication and advertising play a key role in this system that is built around the imaginary.

This business model may have originated in the United States, but some European brands like Armani, Lacoste and Boss adopted it. This category is characterized by its flat and circular model, also called a 'galaxy', in which the center represents the brand ideal.[11] In this model, there is no hierarchy. All the manifestations of the brand, including licenses and extensions, are more or less equidistant from the center. They all portray the brand and its values in an equally important way and thus each extension is treated with the same care. For example, Ralph Lauren launched a range of home decorating paint that was seen as successful because home and decoration are an integral part of the brand's concept and the universe created around this brand. Price differences are smaller than in the first business model and a decrease in the level of creativity is not visible.[12]

7.3 THE LUXURY FASHION BRAND-BUILDING PROCESS

The brand-building process comprises seven steps. The process starts by identifying the brand concept and the brand identity. Brand awareness is then created through actions that increase the visibility of the brand to its target group. When the brand is visible, it needs correct positioning in the consumers' minds. The creation of brand loyalty, brand equity and brand value is the last step in the luxury brand-building process (Figure 7.1).

7.3.1 Brand concept

The brand concept is the overall idea behind the creation of the brand.[13] The name of the brand, the history and/or story of the brand, its country-of-origin, the visual image of the brand, its logo, colors, shapes, language used and its total offerings reflect the brand concept. These elements help to convey a luxury, premium or prestige brand image.[14]

When comparing the brand concepts of luxury brands, one can see that different luxury brands have distinct brand concepts, but they generally share similar characteristics of 'prestige'.[15] Products take a preponderant place, like watches for Rolex, handbags for Hermès and the *tailleur* for Chanel.[16] The Hermès logo contains a horse carriage that refers to its history, the color orange is used for its packaging and advertisements are in French. Louis Vuitton chose brown as the color of its packaging while Tiffany & Co. chose blue and Burberry created its tartan, a recognizable motif.

The name of most luxury brands refers to their founder, or to the most important designer, and often gives an indication of the country of origin. [17] However, there are exceptions. The Italian JP Tods chose its name from the telephone directory because of its ease of pronunciation in different languages. This name was also in line with the brand concept, namely to translate the American

FIGURE 7.1 **The brand building process**

casual style through Italian luxury know-how into luxury weekend fashion.[18]

Many luxury brands are nowadays changing their names. Dior dropped the word 'Christian' and other brands start to use initials like 'LV' for Louis Vuitton and 'YSL' for Yves Saint Laurent. At the same time, the logos of various luxury brands are being modernized, while others stick to their logo as it reflects their heritage, like Hermès. Other brands like Bottega Veneta rely on the signature of their products as recognizable tools and minimize the logos on their products.[19]

7.3.2 Brand identity

The brand identity is the branding element that is developed after the establishment of the brand concept. It reflects who the brand truly is and how the brand is perceived by the consumers. The brand identity can be split into two components: the brand personality and the brand image.[20]

The brand personality can be defined as how the brand wants to be seen by others. It is thus how the company wants the brand to be perceived. The personality of a brand is important in order to position the brand accurately in the minds of the consumers. In order to project the right image, the brand personality should be clear and consistent. The company will lose market share if the brand identity is not well defined as consumers will be confused. At the same time, it must be memorable and affirmative, and must distinguish the brand from competing brands. The brand identity should focus on the points of differentiation that deliver sustainable competitive advantage to the company. The brand identity should also reflect the company's strategy. It is the foundation of all activities that can be designed as being manifestations of the brand, for example, products, advertisement campaigns and the architectural concept of stores.[21] Luxury brands share certain brand personality traits like reliance, glamour, originality and sophistication, but luxury brands also exhibit different traits that make the brand unique.[22]

The brand image reflects the way the brand is perceived by consumers and prospects that are exposed to the brand. The brand image is therefore an interpretation of the brand. In fact, rather than brand image, it would be more accurate to speak about brand images, because different consumers or prospects may interpret the brand in different ways. Brands whose image contains 'heritage' and 'authenticity' are more appealing to consumers because they are more likely to succeed in the creation of emotional and symbolic attachment. The brand image is the most precious position of a luxury company since it is the ticket to an exceptional or ideal universe.[23]

Luxury brands are already perceived by their consumers and prospects as 'luxury'. This gives the brands an advantage in the development of the brand personality and brand image. It is the reason why luxury brands do not need the slogans or characters that are very often found in other brand categories to support the brand symbols.[24]

7.3.3 Brand awareness

Awareness means that there is a high level of knowledge about the brand, or consciousness of its existence.[25] Brand awareness can be measured as the ability of consumers to identify the brand under different conditions. It consists of two elements, namely brand recognition and brand recall performance. Brand recognition is the consumer's ability to confirm prior exposure to the brand when the brand is being shown. Brand recall performance refers to the consumer's ability to recall the brand when the product category, the need fulfilled by this category, a purchase or a usage situation is given.[26]

Luxury fashion brands generally generate higher levels of awareness compared to mass fashion brands since they are seen as more aspirational and unique because of the 'luxury' element. The luxury fashion goods market is also smaller than the mass luxury market and focuses on a global market, which makes it easier for luxury brands to stand out. Nevertheless, the task of creating brand awareness becomes more challenging because of changes in the market, namely the lowering of the sector's entry costs and subsequent expansions.[27]

Brand awareness is achieved through the creation of visibility. This means that its target consumer audience is highly exposed to the brand. A high visibility is important but one needs to be careful not to over-expose the consumers. The challenge therefore is to stay visible while maintaining exclusivity – *placing the brand to be seen, heard and thought about by the right people with the aim of registering the brand in their memory.*[28] In the luxury world, to become a tasteful product one needs talent, inspiration, but also recognition from clients whose choice influences the opinion of others.[29] Awareness can, in this case, be generated using celebrity endorsement.

Awareness can also be created using marketing tools such as advertising, sales promotions, sponsorship, public relations but also by word-of-mouth. Additionally, thanks to the global reach of the Internet, websites can boost awareness. Furthermore, the increase in international travel and the emergence of the global market place are rapidly boosting awareness.[30]

7.3.4 Brand positioning

Brand positioning is described as the act of designing the company's offer and image so that it occupies a distinct and valued place in the target customer's minds. Positioning is therefore about finding the right 'location' in the mind of a consumer, a consumer group or a market segment so that they think about a product or service in the desired way. The connection between a brand and the consumer's mind and emotions is thus emphasized by brand positioning. It articulates why a consumer should choose a specific brand over another.[31] Good positioning helps to maximize the potential benefits of a company. It guides the marketing strategy since it clarifies what the brand is all about, how unique it is, what similarities there are with competing brands and why consumers should buy and use it.[32]

The positioning of luxury brands occurs on two levels: a broad and a narrow level of positioning. Broad positioning is easily and effectively achieved by luxury brands. It is characterized by high-end, expensive and well-crafted products, and thus is the positioning that most luxury brands wish to occupy. Narrow positioning is about specific brand positioning and therefore is unique for different brands. The own positioning of each brand is supported by its brand identity. At this point, the battle for consumers begins because brand positioning is what drives consumer choices through comparisons.[33]

Two choices must be made while positioning a product. The first choice is about price. The manufacturer can choose between a low-cost, premium or prestige strategy. When opting for the prestige strategy, the price will give exclusivity to the brand that is not only related to the quality of the product but also to the target group. The second choice is based on immaterial and material aspects around the brand, such as an experience world that can be created around it. Marketing communication will play an important role here.[34]

When it comes to luxury, what really matters is being unique. Marketers have to forget about brand positioning and put their effort into the definition of brand identity. *Luxury is the expression of a taste, of a creative identity, of the intrinsic passion of the creator; luxury makes the bald statement, 'this is what I am', not 'it depends'– which is what positioning implies.*[35]

7.3.5 Brand loyalty, brand equity and brand value

Brand loyalty, brand equity and brand value are the last three steps in the luxury brand-building process. Brand loyalty is the consumer's preference for a brand in a certain product category. The success and the relevance of branding are shown by brand loyalty. Luxury consumers are often highly emotionally attached to the brand and very loyal. For outsiders, their love for the brand can even seem irrational. The relationship between a customer and a brand often shifts from functionality to symbolism because the brand helps to project a self-image. The consumer uses luxury goods to show other people the person they are or aspire to be. Luxury goods thus become communication tools.[36]

Brand equity is what gives the consumer a reason to prefer certain brands and their underlying products over alternative products of alternative brands of which they are aware. It is the sum of all the distinctive qualities of a brand that result in the continuous demand and commitment of customers to the brand. Brand equity leads to brand value.

Brand value is the final result of the success or failure of the brand. Brand value is generated at the end of the brand-building process and all the different steps contribute to it. Brand value differs from brand equity as brand equity is based on consumer psychological indicators, whereas brand value is the translation of this equity into financial gains for the company that owns the brand.[37]

The biggest part of the brand value is generated by the imaginary. It is so strong that some believe that it is the most important factor in calculating the value of the brand. They say that 90 percent of the stock value of Hermès is composed by the six letters of its name and that only 10 percent reflects its workshops and primary resources, namely its tangible assets.[38]

7.4 THE KEY CHARACTERISTICS OF A LUXURY BRAND

Luxury brands are one of the purest examples of branding. The brand and its image are key competitive advantages and create enormous value and wealth. Without branding, luxury goods would not be as appealing or would not even exist.[39]

Research relevant to the creation and development of luxury brands is rather limited. The research about luxury brands that has been conducted so far mainly focused on motivations for purchasing luxury goods and brand extensions. Recently, researchers started to consider the dimensions of luxury brands. Here we focus on the nine key characteristics as identified by Fionda and Moore.[40]

Figure 7.2 illustrates the various dimensions or characteristics that are inherent in luxury fashion brands. All the characteristics are interdependent and must be managed simultaneously to achieve luxury status. The characteristics will be exposed in the following sections and illustrated by the results of a case study of six traditional leather goods brands: Bottega Veneta, Delvaux, Hermès, Loewe, Louis Vuitton and Prada. The brands have the same characteristics but do not give the same weight to each of them. This shows the path-dependent nature of the creation and development of luxury leather goods brands, and luxury brands in general.

The House of Delvaux, a Belgian luxury leather goods manufacturer, realized that brands had become more important than the products and that the development of the brand would be essential to remain successful.[41] Traditional leather goods manufacturers that had focused for years on the products therefore had to

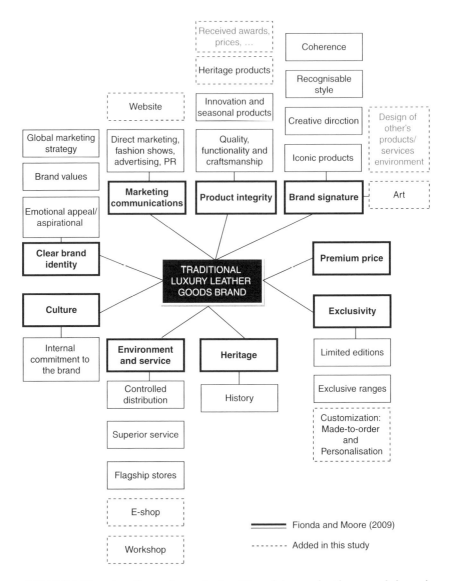

FIGURE 7.2 **The nine dimensions of a traditional, luxury leather goods brand (Fionda and Moore's model revised)**

adapt themselves. Brands are today the products that are consumed and the products no longer speak for themselves. Brand building becomes a priority when the brand becomes more important than the product or service itself.

Throughout the history of Delvaux and Hermès, one can see that the companies have adapted their products and themselves to the changing needs (e.g. changing modes of traveling – boat, train, car or changing lifestyles – working women) and market conditions. The fit with social trends and the spirit of the time are crucial aspects for a luxury goods company.[42]

The companies also started to widen their product ranges, by offering products in categories that were new to them such as clothing and jewelry. Selling accessories is no longer enough for companies such as Bottega Veneta, Loewe and Dunhill.[43] A designer brand must touch every aspect of the lives of its customers.

7.4.1 Clear brand identity

A global marketing strategy, brand values, emotional and aspirational appeal are the elements that define a clear brand identity. Products that have a strong aspirational appeal are bought not just because they are well-crafted or have an exceptional quality, but also because of the prestigious image they generate. They are bought to acquire a piece of the brand's heritage. Brand values must be clear and must make the brand different and relevant in the current marketplace. The company must have plans to develop the brand through various investments to guarantee the brand's future.[44]

7.4.1.1 Illustration

All six luxury leather goods brands have clearly defined brand values that form part of their identity. Creativity, craftsmanship, functionality and innovation are the most important values. A good knowledge of these values throughout the organization is essential.

Delvaux adopts the same marketing strategy around the world. The company wants to continue to promote itself as a luxury leather goods company. Therefore, Delvaux will continue to emphasize its know-how, craftsmanship, historic creativity and its origins. Its distribution strategy abroad is slightly different because it mainly operates abroad through third parties such as department stores. Bottega Veneta's retail concept is not standardized.

The company wants its stores to reflect the current city and its architectural characteristics while keeping the values and image of the brand in mind. Architecture is for Louis Vuitton a passion that makes every store unique.

Hermès sells such a large number of products because it makes people dream. The brands need to have an emotional appeal or satisfy some of the customer's aspirations.

7.4.2 Marketing communications

Powerful marketing communications are the key to building the image of the luxury brand. This image helps in the creation of the identity and the attraction as well as in the generation of awareness. The beautiful and selective quality of the product must be communicated.[45]

Other means of luxury brand communication are public relations, celebrity endorsement, events, direct marketing, sponsorship, fashion shows but also blogs, press, the store as a communication tool and personal communication.[46]

7.4.2.1 Illustration

Delvaux, Hermès, Bottega Veneta, Loewe, Prada and Louis Vuitton all invest in marketing communications and especially in public relations (PR), direct marketing and advertising. The companies present their collections by organizing fashion shows.

Celebrity endorsement and the use of celebrities in advertising campaigns to create more awareness are practiced by some brands, Loewe and Louis Vuitton for example. Others, on the other hand, such as Bottega Veneta and Hermès, choose not to, believing that it has no effect on brand awareness.

The brand's website is not always seen as a major communication tool;[47] however, all companies do have a website and invest in it. People can subscribe to newsletters, personalize the website and discover the company's universe and values.

One-to-one marketing is gaining importance, and luxury brands are investing in it as direct communication with the customer on a personal level is becoming more important. Nonetheless, Louis

Vuitton entered the world of cinema and television with their 'where will life take you?' commercial.

7.4.3 Product integrity

The quality of products is objective and fragile.[48] Being flawless is the aim of a premium product, but not of a luxury product. Flaws can be seen as charming and as a guarantee of authenticity.[49] The quality must meet or exceed the customer's expectations and therefore the company must achieve a relative flawless value delivery. Quality is ensured by the best materials and craftsmanship. Since the 1980s, some luxury brands have focused more on the symbolic at the expense of the functional. Material quality declined, skilled craftsmen made place for outsourced mass production but the fantasy world around brands like Prada became more attractive than ever.[50]

Fashion companies have both classical products and innovative or seasonal products in their collection. Creativity and innovation are seen as a key characteristic.[51] Innovation is a way to remain a reference on the market. Thus, innovative products are needed to keep the brand fresh and exciting, while classical pieces reflect the brand's heritage. Furthermore, vintage reflects authenticity and incorporates nostalgia.[52]

7.4.3.1 Illustration

Quality, attention-to-detail, handmade and craftsmanship are characteristics of the luxury leather goods companies. Quality is not only assured by the manufacturing of the goods, but also by the superior quality of raw materials. Therefore, good relationships with suppliers are crucial. Hermès went further and bought some of its suppliers. To ensure quality, a limited number of craftsmen can work on a handbag. Some companies started their own school or partnerships with schools to train leather workers and craftsmen.

Creativity is important in fashion. When it comes to leather goods, the product offer is divided into heritage products – products that remain longer in the collection – and seasonal products.

Heritage products often remain in the collection for many years. Seasonal products, on the other hand, stay in the product offer only a few seasons and are characterized by a higher level of creativity and innovation. The collections are therefore balanced. The leather goods sector relies more heavily on permanent offers than does the ready-to-wear sector.[53] Products must in the first place be functional and therefore will need to be adjusted throughout the years to match the current social trends, transportation methods and so on.

Awards and prizes also contribute to product integrity. Delvaux and Loewe are recognized suppliers of the royal family. Hermès was awarded a quality medal for its work as a saddler in 1867. Delvaux actively uses this 'award' in its communication and logo.

7.4.4 Brand signature

Luxury brands can create recognizable styles, products and motifs.[54] All the products of a brand should be consistent and coherent. Iconic products are central to the luxury product offering. These are typified by authenticity, quality and exclusive characteristics, and are aspirational. The appointment of high-profile fashion designers enhances the products' appeal.[55]

7.4.4.1 Illustration

The importance of a recognizable style and iconic products also concerns luxury leather goods brands. Bottega Veneta reflects 'when your initials are sufficient', while Louis Vuitton's monogram is on almost all the products. The brands have iconic products. The Knot is the iconic product of Bottega Veneta and Le Brillant of Delvaux. For Hermès, the coherence of its style is one of its strengths. Made-to-measure products are created by Louis Vuitton taking into account the esthetics of the brand.

The companies employ creative directors and designers that have already proven themselves. Hermès differs slightly from the other brands because its creative director is a family member. Nevertheless, it has other designers working for the brand.

The packaging of the company must be coherent with the company image. While not all the companies have recognizable packaging, Hermès does. The companies design for, or together with, other companies – cars, hotel rooms and bathtubs, for example.

Art is linked to creativity, innovation and craftsmanship. Hermès organizes the 'Prix Emile Hermès', a design award. Loewe has a foundation in its name that supports poetry, music, design and craftsmanship. Louis Vuitton has worked with various artists such as the Japanese artist, Takashi Murakami, and the graffiti artist, Stephen Spouse. The brand also has a foundation in its name, the Fondation Louis Vuitton. Prada, with its Fondazione Prada, initially supported contemporary art, and later added architecture, philosophy, science and design. Luxury products do not only want to sell their products but they also want to sell an image that makes the difference. The image from the brand rests on both the exceptional quality of the product and its relationship with art.[56]

7.4.5 Premium prices

Expensive products cannot be defined as luxury products. Price is nevertheless an essential part of the brand as it confirms the strategic positioning. The price of luxury goods should be based on the imaginary, not on the costs.[57] Luxury products have the highest price/quality ratio or premium prices, but what matters are higher relative prices. Price contributes to the luxury status and increases exclusivity. Luxury brands give therefore few discounts and markdowns.[58]

7.4.5.1 *Illustration*

The products of the luxury leather goods brands have premium prices. Behind these prices hide the high manufacturing costs of the products, for example, wages in developed countries and superior quality of materials. Some brands argue that their margins are lower than those of other luxury companies because of the reasons mentioned above. Evidence is found that some brands do give price reductions and organize outlet sales, but not in their shops. Some of the brands also manufacture particular product ranges abroad to cut costs and to have sufficient resources to ensure their competitiveness.

7.4.6 Exclusivity

Rarity and exclusivity are both seen as dimensions of a luxury brand. The non-availability of the brand is important.[59] This can be translated into limited editions, exclusive ranges[60] and the use of waiting lists.[61] Rarity has more than one manifestation.[62] While rarity might influence the buying intentions made by Western consumers, it is less relevant to Asian consumers.[63]

7.4.6.1 Illustration

The companies ensure exclusivity by carefully selecting the distribution channels, as well as through limited production runs, or waiting lists. Special editions or collector items are made for special events, and customization is offered. Customers can ask to have their product personalized or order a tailor-made one. Personalizing is part of the customization process and currently is one of the key requirements.[64] Most brands have their own distribution network and therefore fully control the accessibility.

7.4.7 Heritage

The long history of a brand adds to the authenticity and creates nostalgia and credibility. It becomes a comparative advantage. The history relates to the history of the country-of-origin.[65] Heritage is also referred to when talking about seniority[66] or 'plundering the past'.[67]

7.4.7.1 Illustration

The companies, with the exception of Bottega Veneta, have a long history going back to the nineteenth century. Most companies stay true to the strategic positioning of that time. Bottega Veneta once lost track and started to manufacture handbags with big logos, but changed again to its initial positioning. Staying true helps to maintain the brand's authenticity.

Their history is used actively by certain brands. Hermès, for example, uses a horse carriage in its logo that refers back to its beginning years, while Delvaux and Prada each make reference to their founding year, 'since 1829' and 'dal 1913' respectively. All product designs of Delvaux are drawn in two books called the 'Gold Books'. Some brands like Louis Vuitton and Prada do not publish their full history on their website but refer to 'their rich past' in various sections.

7.4.8 Environment and service

The environment and experience of the brand are showcased in the flagship stores.[68] The physical environment must differ from that of its competition.[69] The design studio and manufacturing plant can also be added to the environment.[70] Further, control over the distributors, suppliers, manufacturers and licensees is crucial.

The choice of the distribution channel is very important as it reflects the brand's values. The use of different distribution channels reinforces the brand's notoriety.[71] Retail distribution is highly selective and controlled because of the highly targeted market segments involved, and the need for exclusivity and prestige.[72] The aim is to protect consumers from non-consumers.[73]

7.4.8.1 Illustration

Superior services, the store environment and control over them are seen as important. The flagship stores are very valuable. Not only is the interior of these stores chosen with care but their location is also of major importance. The companies opened stores in key fashion cities and neighborhoods.

These stores are characterized by their enormous surface and their design by well-known architects. The full collection is exposed, but the stores are not always standardized or fully operated by the companies themselves. Most of the case companies own franchise stores and some sell products through high-end department stores or specialist boutiques.

The case companies emphasize the importance of staff training. About Bottega Veneta was written 'our stores are our way to communicate and our sales staff must know our history, our techniques and workmanship, the materials and the crafts and transmit it to the customers'.[74] Delvaux made a brochure containing this information for newly hired staff and trains its sales staff. Bottega Veneta, Delvaux and Hermès also offer a limited range of their products on their e-shops. E-retail has become an indispensible complementary sales channel.[75] The workshops of some of the companies are opened for guided visits.

7.4.9 Culture

Internal and external commitment can be extended by the investment in the culture of the company. Actors from inside and outside the company will support the brand.[76] Leading companies understand that an internal culture that supports the brand strategy has a better chance of delivering a relevant, consistent, yet differentiated experience. The concept of an 'employer brand', the image of the brand through the eyes of potential and current employees has been introduced. Its aim is to retain and attract the best employees. There is, in general, a strong correlation between the way that employers perceive and feel about the brand and the way customers view it. *Those who live the brand, will deliver the brand.*[77]

The company also needs external commitment from its partners. Therefore, the right choice of manufacturers and licensees is important.[78] Currently, there is a trend to widen involvement to all stakeholders.[79]

7.4.9.1 *Illustration*

During the research, little information was found regarding the internal and external commitment to the brand. Nevertheless, concerning internal commitment there is one example from Hermès. The company gives stock options to its craftsmen. Concerning external commitment, a good relationship with suppliers had been identified as being crucial to ensuring the good quality of the raw materials.

7.5 CONCLUSION

Over the years, brands have become more important than the products. Traditional luxury companies have had to adapt themselves to this new condition in order to remain relevant and successful. Having superior products was no longer their customers' most important priority. It was suddenly all about products having the right image. Brands had to be developed without touching the specificities.

Two major business models have been developed over the years. Both business models have different approaches toward brands and brand building. While the first business model puts the emphasis on the product, the second concentrates much more on the image.

The luxury brand-building process has been seen to contain seven steps. First, the brand concept and the brand identity have to be defined. Later, brand awareness is created by increasing the visibility of the brand. When the brand is visible to its target group, the brand should get the positioning in the consumer's mind. The creation of brand loyalty, brand equity and brand value are the final steps in the luxury brand building process.

The chapter then presented the nine characteristics of a luxury fashion brand. These characteristics were further illustrated by the results of a case study including six traditional luxury leather goods brands. All these characteristics must be managed simultaneously in order to achieve luxury status. These dimensions are interdependent. The importance that is given to each of the characteristics varies and this shows the path-dependent nature of the creation and development of luxury brands.

8

BRAND EXTENSIONS IN THE LUXURY INDUSTRY

Rasa Stankeviciute

8.1 INTRODUCTION

Brand extensions are an interesting brand strategy alternative, as they may attract new segments of customers who, for various reasons, may have not considered the luxury brand before. The luxury brand extensions have gained such momentum that today a fan of a luxury fashion house is able not only to dress herself from head to toe in a beloved designer's clothes, but also serve dinner in the same designer's porcelain dinnerware or simply dine in the restaurant under the same designer's name (Ralph Lauren, for example). The American luxury jewelry brand Tiffany & Co., long known for fulfilling every woman's dreams by offering high-end jewelry and high-quality silver accessories in the iconic blue box, decided to try gaining more business by extending the brand into watches, handbags and briefcases. Some luxury fashion brands, like Gucci and Stella McCartney, have joined many others, like Burberry and Ralph Lauren, in targeting children (or their fashion-conscious mothers) by offering children's wear lines – a popular luxury fashion brand extension.

As diversification of the luxury brands has reached such heights, and the number of luxury lifestyle brands is increasing so rapidly, it would make no sense to continue to talk about how important it is to extend the luxury brands into adjacent categories in order not to dilute them. Today, companies must find other ways to avoid brand extension mistakes and to ensure that brand extensions will not dilute the brand with a well-established name for luxury.

8.2 WHAT DOES BRAND EXTENSION STAND FOR?

Many authors have introduced their own definitions of brand extensions (see Table 8. 1), even though at the end of the day, everyone refers to the same result – introducing new products in order for the company to grow. There is, however, always a slight risk of confusion when talking about the brand extensions. Aaker[1] describes *brand extension* as the use of a brand name established in one product class to enter another product class (e. g. Armani Casa furnishings), while describing *line extensions* as offering new products within the same category (such as the Emporio Armani fashion line). Kapferer[2] warns that *line extension* should be differentiated from the *brand extension*, as the latter is 'a real diversification toward different product categories and different clients'. However, this definition can be questioned, as, for instance, if we look at the Armani brand, it is quite obvious that with Armani Dolci, Armani Flowers or even Armani Hotels, the parent luxury brand targets the same fashion-conscious customers that it targets with its fashion lines, though the product categories of these extensions are very different from the apparel.

Meanwhile, Best[3] classifies the ways of introducing new products into *horizontal* brand extensions and *vertical* brand extensions. Thus

TABLE 8.1 **Different definitions of brand extensions by author**

	Farquhar (1989)	**Aaker (1991)**	**Kapferer (2008)**	**Best (2009)**
New product launched in the same category as the parent brand (e.g. Emporio Armani fashion line)	Line extension	Line extension	Line extension	Vertical brand extension
New product launched in other category than the parent brand (e.g. Armani Casa furnishings)	Category extension	Brand extension	Brand extension	Horizontal brand extension

Best's classification endorses what could be regarded as the clearest definition so far of brand extensions, one provided by Farquhar in 1989.[4] Farquhar classified all brand extensions into two broad categories: *line extensions* and *category extensions*. A *line extension* exists when 'the parent brand is used to brand a new product that targets a new market segment within a product category currently served by the parent brand'. A *category extension,* on the other hand, exists when 'the parent brand is used to enter a different product category from that currently served by the parent brand'. To be clear, we would suggest referring to Farquhar's classification, while keeping in mind that every use of a parent brand to introduce a new product is brand extension.

8.3 LUXURY BRAND EXTENSIONS

Brand extensions were initiated in the luxury goods industry, when luxury fashion houses originating in *haute couture* started extending to jewelry, accessories, watches and cosmetics.[5] French luxury fashion houses were the first to start selling their brand name perfume as brand extensions. Chanel launched its first perfume *Chanel No 5* in 1921, and it remains one of the best-selling perfumes in the world.

While companies see brand extensions as the perfect way to increase revenues, researchers see them as a perfect field for investigation. Today, brand extensions are one of the most heavily researched and influential areas in marketing.[6] However, the majority of brand extension research has focused on non-luxury brands and much of the research is far removed from the real context of the luxury brands, or has particular limitations.[7] Thus, there is still a very broad field for investigation for companies wishing to attract and satisfy wealthy potential consumers.

Brand extensions in the luxury sector can positively impact the parent brand if adequate consideration is given to some key issues. These include diversification, non-luxury partner choice, downward brand extension, entrance to new markets and constant innovation in the core business. The four case studies that follow present different practices of brand extensions by well-known brands (see Table 8. 2).

TABLE 8.2 **Brands analyzed**

Brand	Rolls-Royce	Mercedes-Benz	Jimmy Choo	Giorgio Armani
Brand extension practice	Downward brand extension	Entrance to new markets	Non-luxury partner choice	Diversification

8.3.1 Downward brand extension enhancing the parent luxury brand – the case of Rolls-Royce

Downward brand extension refers to the introduction of a lower-end product line positioned at a lower price than other product lines of the luxury parent brand. Even though the downward brand extension is usually directed toward new segments of customers, those, for example, who cannot afford the more expensive product, the luxury brand has, nevertheless, to offer a product that has luxury criteria (outstanding quality, uniqueness, scarcity, exclusive distribution, carefully selected points-of-sale, high price, history and heritage) and which corresponds to the qualities and values of the parent luxury brand. In this way, the downward brand extension may enhance the parent luxury brand instead of diluting it. The UK-based Rolls-Royce introduces a story of real luxury and success.

In the end of 2009, Rolls-Royce expanded downwards by launching a new, cheaper car model, the Ghost. According to Tom Purves, the former CEO of Rolls-Royce Motor Cars, Rolls-Royce's customers could still afford the £300,000 asking price for the Phantom model, but some buyers did not feel it was the right time to spend on such conspicuous symbol of wealth.[8] Such clients' unwillingness to spend money forces the companies to have downward brand extensions, and this is most likely the reason Rolls-Royce introduced a car model in a different price category. When the Ghost was introduced, customer deliveries were available for €213,000 for the base model compared to €345,700 for the Phantom base model.

The downward brand extensions help companies reach a wider audience of potential customers. The Ghost was meant to reach the customers who prefer 'the power of simplicity' to the 'sense of scale and occasion', offered by the Phantom model. Evidently, the

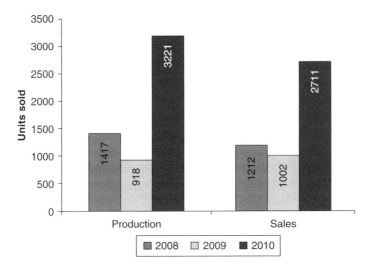

CHART 8.1 **Rolls-Royce total production and sales**
Source: Rolls-Royce Motor Cars data

brand extension brought an impressive number of new customers to the brand (see Chart 8.1), as around 80 percent of the customers of the Ghost model had never previously owned a Rolls-Royce.[9] That means that the Ghost did provide name recognition and associations to new segments – the advantage of line extensions considered by Aaker.[10]

Nevertheless, downward brand extensions can dilute the parent luxury brand if they fail to correspond to the brand's qualities and values, and do not possess the luxury criteria. Thus, it was crucial for the people behind the Rolls-Royce brand to make sure that the Ghost proved the qualities and values of the luxury parent brand, and did not have a chance to fail and so weaken its image in any way. Indeed, according to Rolls-Royce Motor Cars, the Ghost is the most technologically advanced Rolls-Royce ever built that redefines not only the brand, but the luxury car market as well. Like the Phantom, the Ghost is hand-built and it shares paint, wood and leather workshops with the Phantom series. According to Mr Ferraiolo, former president of Rolls-Royce Motor Cars North America, despite the lower price, the Ghost 'has all the attributes of a Rolls-Royce, but with less size'.[11] Tom Ford of *Top Gear Magazine* endorsed the statement, by adding, 'it is the Ghost's [...] utter confidence of character that allows it to use BMW bits and still produce undeniably a Rolls – that makes it such a success'.[12] Moreover, the prestigious red dot awards honored the Ghost with awards for outstanding product design and highest design quality.

In 2010, Rolls-Royce Motor Cars more than tripled the production figures and more than doubled the sales figures compared to 2009 (see Chart 8.1). The Ghost model accounted for the sales of 2174 automobiles (80 percent) out of 2711 (see Charts 8.2 and 8.3), and the Ghost model's continued success made the company increase the size of the Leathershop team in order to meet the growing demands of the customers.

Evidently, this downward brand extension has enhanced the parent luxury brand. Nevertheless, even successful brand extensions can be risky, as brand extensions can cannibalize sales of the parent brand if consumers decide to switch from existing brand offerings to the brand extension.[13] Unfortunately, the extension's sales

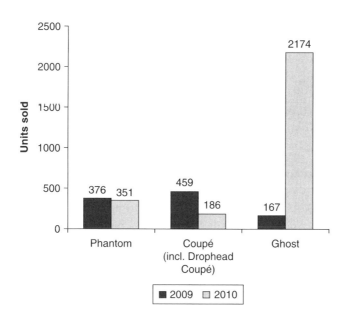

CHART 8.2 **Rolls-Royce sales by model**
Source: Rolls-Royce Motor Cars data

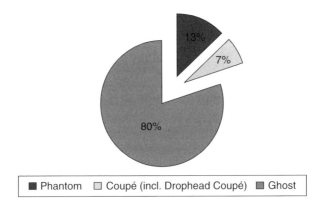

CHART 8.3 **Each model's input in 2010 sales**
Source: Rolls-Royce Motor Cars data

cannot compensate such impact on parent brand's customer loyalty and damage to the original brand's equity.[14]

Although in 2010 the sales of the Phantom and Phantom Coupé cars did drop by 7 percent and 59 percent accordingly, the Ghost would have hardly cannibalized the sales of its predecessors, as only 20 percent of the customers who bought the Ghost model were not new to the brand. Instead, the contrary may happen: after experiencing the qualities of the Rolls-Royce Ghost, which clearly corresponds to the qualities and values of the parent brand, the new customers may later switch to the more expensive offerings of the luxury brand.

8.3.2 From luxury to premium – the case of Mercedes-Benz

Mercedes-Benz – arguably considered a premium, no longer a luxury, the German automobile brand has introduced a different brand extension practice from that experienced by the Rolls-Royce brand. By launching A-Class – a downward brand extension (a Mercedes for around €20,000) in 1997 – the brand entered a different market from most of its current markets worldwide.[15] The entrance was not successful, as the safety test revealed defects in the car's stability and so harmed the image of Mercedes-Benz as one of the most secure cars of that time. The delivery of the A-Class cars was suspended and the security problems were fixed, but then this brand extension resulted in 'the weakening of Mercedes' status through the commercial success of the A-Class'.[16] In 1998, 136,100 units of the A-Class were sold,[17] followed by 207,000 units sold in 1999.[18] The car failed to correspond to the luxury criteria, such as limited accessibility and high price, as it became too accessible because of its reasonable good quality and small price ratio. In contrast, the price of the Rolls-Royce Ghost, though lower than that of the Phantom, is too high for the model to become too accessible.

On top of the issues faced by the A-Class model, problems of quality were frequent in many other brand extensions of Mercedes-Benz. In 2004, the brand recalled 680,000 cars equipped with an advanced braking system that had been sold as revolutionary, but which then showed tendencies to fail.[19] In 2005, 1.3 million cars were recalled because of electronic bugs, further damaging the brand name with bad quality, especially because the main troublesome problems with the electronics were in the luxurious Mercedes E-Class.[20]

With all these failures, today the Mercedes brand is no longer perceived as a luxury car maker in the United States: it has lost the power of dreams, one of the criteria for the luxury brand.[21] European consumers, on the other hand, seem to have a slightly different opinion on this point. Wealthy European consumers rated Mercedes-Benz the second most prestigious European luxury automobile brand (after Porsche) in the 2009 Luxury Brand Status Index survey from Luxury Institute.[22] Then again, for some reason, neither Rolls-Royce nor Bentley was included in the list of choices.

8.3.3 Diversification of the brand – the case of Giorgio Armani

Armani is probably the most diversified brand of the fashion and luxury industries (see Table 8.3). Despite wide expansions into different sectors, such as hospitality (Armani Hotels) or home furnishings (Armani Casa), clothing, accounting for 59 percent of turnover in 2009,[23] remains the core business of the brand. Armani targets every segment of fashion consumers by offering clothing labels ranging from haute couture, with Armani Privé, to fast fashion with Armani Exchange, at a number of different price-points.

TABLE 8.3 Armani brand architecture

GIORGIO ARMANI

Luxury → Fast fashion (spectrum, top to bottom)

Women's Fashion	Men's Fashion	Children's Fashion	Jewelry	Watches	Eyewear	Beauty	Home	Services	Others
Armani Privé	Hand Made-To-Measure Giorgio Armani		Armani Privé Fine Jewelry			Armani Privé Fragrances	Armani Casa	Armani Hotels & Resorts Armani SPA	Armani Samsung TV
Giorgio Armani	Giorgio Armani		GA Costume Jewelry	Giorgio Armani	Giorgio Armani	GA Beauty (Cosmetics, Fragrances)		Armani Ristorante Armani Bar	GA Samsung Smart Phone
Armani Collezioni	Armani Collezioni								
Emporio Armani (incl. EA7)	Emporio Armani (incl. EA7)		EA Costume Jewelry	Emporio Armani	Emporio Armani	EA Fragrances		EA Caffè	EA Samsung Mobile
Armani Jeans	Armani Jeans	Armani Baby Armani Junior Armani Teen						AJ Caffè	
Armani Exchange	Armani Exchange		AX Costume Jewelry	Armani Exchange	Armani Exchange				Armani Dolci Armani Fiori Armani Libri

Ledbury Research found that once people relate the brand with lower-end goods, it is difficult to move up-market and attract the target segment of the top-luxury brand.[24] Therefore, it is a huge risk for the luxury brand to launch a fast fashion label. However, since Armani Exchange – called 'accessible Armani' by the brand itself – was launched in 1991, its parent luxury brand has been far from being related with lower-end goods. According to Clifton,[25] it is perfectly possible to manage downward extensions alongside the premium brands when providing the value range that still feels like good quality, and when the main brand continues to innovate and present the kind of quality experience that is valued by loyal customers. Indeed, the Armani group makes sure that each brand, positioned to different segments of customers, is distinguishable. One could never find Armani Exchange accessories sold in the same points-of-sale as the other Armani brand accessories, and Armani Exchange is absent from the Armani concept stores. Moreover, despite the low price compared to other Armani lines, Armani Exchange is expensive for its segment; while higher-end brands offer the kind of quality experience, such as shipping a Armani Collezioni coat of requested size from Milan to Paris in a couple of days, that is expected and valued by the loyal customers. All Armani brands have uniquely designed store interiors for that one particular brand. Furthermore, all Armani fashion lines remain creative with innovative textile research and each brand's own variation on the common spirit on the Armani website.[26] Nevertheless, every brand represents the philosophy of Armani and corresponds to the unique Armani style.

Although the Italian designer has been successful so far in every venture he has done, the Armani brand might face difficulties because of over-extension. By extending into many other sectors than fashion, the Armani brand may lose an instant identification with fashion category. 'The potential drawbacks from a lack of identification with any one category and a weakened image may be especially evident with high quality or prestige brands.'[27] Therefore, the lack of instant identification with the fashion category may weaken the Armani brand image and dilute the luxury brand. According to Interbrand,[28] the diversification sets Armani up for the risk of brand dilution, especially during a recession. When facing financial issues, consumers of luxury goods do not stop buying, but

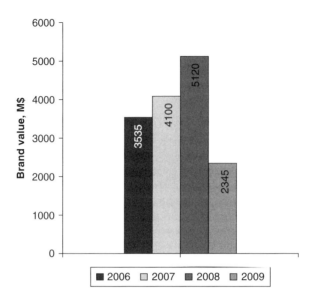

CHART 8.4 **Armani brand value change**
Source: Millward Brown Optimor and BrandZ data

start looking at them as a long-term investment; therefore choosing the luxury brands with the highest status index. In the Millward Brown Optimor rankings of luxury brands according to their brand value, Armani fell out of the top ten in 2009 with the brand value of $2.3 billion compared to the brand value of $5.12 billion in 2008 (see Chart 8.4). The brand did not get back into the top ten in 2010, as well as in 2011.

According to Millward Brown Optimor, Armani brand extensions change the image of the brand, as the extensions into luxury lifestyle businesses, other than fashion, not only enable the Armani brand to grow, but also reinforce its image as a lifestyle provider. Yet, as the Giorgio Armani Group itself presents the Armani brands as the lifestyle brands in the group's annual reports, it is obvious that Mr Armani wants to provide a luxury lifestyle for his clientele and let them feel the unique Armani style in whatever the customers choose. 'In furniture, too, there is glamour and luxury that must be apparent, so that it differentiates itself – and justifies the price tag' – says Mr. Armani.[29] Unfortunately, according to Milton Pedraza of Luxury Institute, Armani's multiple brand extensions, including Armani Exchange, Armani Casa and Armani Hotels, have stretched the brand 'a bit too thin'; therefore 'it's not unique and exclusive anymore'.[30] And while being a luxury lifestyle brand is fine, not being unique and exclusive for the Armani brand would be a problem, as uniqueness and exclusivity are two of the criteria defining the luxury brand. Therefore, notwithstanding the diversification of the luxury brand, its core business has to be constantly enhanced and innovated to keep it exclusive and unique for the brand portfolio to be successful rather than diluted.

8.3.4 Luxury brand extensions within collaboration with a non-luxury brand – the case of Jimmy Choo

Fashion collaborations among luxury and non-luxury brands are currently very popular and very successful, as they may not only intrigue the existing luxury brand's clientele by offering something unexpected, but also attract fashion-conscious customers who cannot afford the luxury brand's offerings. The latter often results during the collaborations between luxury fashion brands and Swedish fast fashion giant H&M. And though it would usually be considered to be a disadvantage for the luxury brand, Tamara Mellon, founder and CCO of Jimmy Choo, is said to be 'privileged to be among the fashion greats who have been affiliated with H&M so far',[31] while Angela Missoni saw such collaborations as a 'very powerful way to reach younger girls now'.[32] True, youth introduced to the luxury brand because of similar collaborations today may become perspective customers of the luxury brand in the future. But while this so far is an assumption, the collaborations among luxury and non-luxury brands can be dangerous, as they may disappoint the loyal clientele of the luxury brand and so damage the luxury brand's image. The extension can succeed or at least survive and damage the brand's perceived quality image or the brand name by creating undesirable attribute associations or by altering or weakening existing brand associations.[33]

Therefore, for the luxury brand to avoid the risk of harming its image, and to boost its clients' excitement and the brand's sales instead, the brand extension within the collaboration with a non-luxury brand has to keep the luxury criteria and the luxury brand's qualities and values, while the non-luxury collaborator has to be respectable and well reputed. Such outcomes were achieved in the Jimmy Choo brand's collaboration with iconic British company Hunter, whose Wellington boots normally cost around £60 a pair, and the collaboration with the maker of iconic sheepskin boots – UGG Australia.

The Jimmy Choo and Hunter's brand extension – luxurious Wellington boots – kept the luxury criteria and the luxury collaborator's values and qualities by having:

- Signature creativity with the signature Jimmy Choo crocodile print, the leopard print lining and gold buckle hardware
- Exclusive distribution with the boots being sold only in Jimmy Choo points-of-sale and official online store
- High price-point for rain boots: $395, €295, £235 for the initial model
- History, quality, durability, comfort and outstanding performance of the iconic Hunter boots.

The Jimmy Choo and UGG Australia brand extension – a limited edition capsule collection – kept the luxury criteria and the luxury collaborator's values and qualities by having:

- The iconic UGG Australia boot construction with recognized quality and expertise
- Jimmy Choo's signature details, such as studding and hobo fringing
- High price-point ranging from £495 to £695
- Exclusive and limited distribution – at selected department stores, Jimmy Choo stores, Jimmy Choo and UGG Australia websites.

Jimmy Choo and Hunter Wellington Boots received a tremendous reaction from customers: the online waiting list opened on 1 May, and by 16 May more than 4000 fashion-conscious customers had already joined it.[34] Today, the luxurious Wellington boots have become a classic item at Jimmy Choo, and can be purchased regardless of the season, and not only in traditional black, but in several variations. According to Hunter Chairman Peter Mullen, the explanation for the success of the collaboration was most likely a strong visual identity of both brands that worked well combined and gave the resulting boot a unique DNA of luxurious practicality.

Apparently, the Jimmy Choo and UGG Australia collection was not less successful, as was the collection for H&M, because according to Mellon, the collaboration with H&M showed that consumers would accept any product from the Jimmy Choo brand, therefore the brand could become the lifestyle brand[35] what Mellon seeks for and sees as an advantage for the brand.

8.3.5 Luxury brand extensions into children's wear market

When the luxury fashion houses noticed that status-conscious parents were willing to dress their children in clothes from the same brands that they wear themselves, or in other words, when the companies understood that there is nothing more satisfying for parents than to spend money on their 'mini-me', luxury brand extensions into the children's wear market gained momentum. But the starting point for many of the brands was the entrance into baby diaper bags (Gucci, Louis Vuitton) or baby gifts (Hermès, Tiffany&Co.) markets, as there had always been someone willing to buy expensive presents for new-borns.

In 2010, children's wear accounted for almost 13 percent, that is €137 billion, of the global apparel, accessories and luxury goods market's total value and it was the third largest segment of the market after the women's wear (40.8 percent) and men's wear (26.4 percent) segments.[36] No wonder the luxury brands see the extensions into children's wear market as a very attractive opportunity to boost the revenues of the company. Children's wear offerings from luxury fashion houses may be considered the New Luxury – 'products [...] that possess higher levels of quality, taste, and aspiration than other goods in the category, but are not so expensive as to be out of reach'.[37] Indeed, according to one Parisian full-time mother and obviously a luxury customer, part of the appeal of buying luxury for children is price, as you can get an outfit for a kid at Dior for €200, whereas for adults you can barely get a T-Shirt for that amount.[38] Naturally, not everyone would consider either the example above or the little boy's two-piece wool suit from Armani Junior for $615 to be not so expensive as to be out of reach. Then again, a parent who can afford a $1,895 suit from Armani Collezioni will probably see no problem in buying a smaller version for his mini-me. Parental narcissism rules here, as, according to Sarah Peters from Verdict Research, parents increasingly see their children as a reflection of themselves, so they want to make sure they look good and are in the latest things.[39]

Besides the revenues that can be generated for the brand, luxury brand extensions into children's wear market may attract new customers to the brand in a long-term. According to James McNeal, the author of several books about marketing to children, brand consciousness begins as young as two years old.[40] Therefore, the brands are hoping that parents will be loyal to the brand and that their children will become the next generation of consumers.[41] And, as the luxury brands are usually willing to invest in the future and cherish the long-term value, it may seem to be a good deal.

Thus, the impact of children's wear lines on the parent luxury brand mainly depends on what approach the companies choose when introducing such extensions. If the children's wear lines remain expensive in accordance with the parent brand's fashion lines for adults and keep the qualities and values of the parent luxury brand, then such extensions could hardly harm the parent luxury brand's image. Conversely, as children's wear brands may be considered a 'new luxury', they may sometimes be judged as inappropriate extensions for such luxury fashion brands that have never before had any downward brand extensions. Consequently, if consumers perceive the extension as inappropriate, they may query the integrity and competence of the brand.[42]

For the Stella McCartney brand's extension into children's wear market, the British fashion designer said, 'I wanted to create a fun, desirable, wearable kid's collection that was affordable' because 'I feel all the timeless children's wear is reserved for the expensive brands and that did not sit well with me'.[43] Yet, Stella McCartney women's wear line is indeed expensive with wool cardigans for $1,095 and coats for $2,595, so why should 'kids and parents, aunts, uncles, friends [....] all be able to have access to Stella McCartney Kids clothes', as claimed by the designer?[44] As has been mentioned in the Armani case, once people relate the brand with lower-end goods, it is difficult to move up-market and attract the target segment of the top-luxury brand. Thus, the customers that are introduced to the Stella McCartney brand through the accessible children's wear line will hardly ever become the parent luxury brand's customers. (The case of the Rolls-Royce brand is different because of the still high price-point for the Ghost model.) And the profits from such brand extension will never outperform the parent luxury brand's profits. Therefore, luxury brand may develop an accessible children's fashion line at the risk of diluting the brand's image.

However, the accessibility of the Stella McCartney Kids line is in fact arguable. Although it is more affordable than the children's wear lines from rival luxury fashion houses, with a T-shirt at $30 or a coat at $124, it is a long way from such brands as H&M or Zara, which are considered to be accessible fashion.

8.4 CONCLUSION

Brand extensions are a never-ending challenge for the luxury brands. They are an important part of the brand's development, so, sooner or later, the companies choose brand extensions in order to grow. The Rolls-Royce brand is one of the best recent examples of how the luxury brand extension attracts a significant number of new costumers to the brand, boosts the sales and makes the company expand. The Armani case raises the question 'What will be next?' as today there can be no limits for diversification. And it would be misleading to think otherwise. What the companies have to understand is that the offerings of the brand extensions must be consistent with the parent brand's qualities and values. Moreover, as the brand extensions often mean moving from the original expertise to the new practice, careful consideration should be given to both the choice of the brand extension and the choice of a partner/collaborator/expert. And finally, no matter how diversified the luxury brand becomes, its core business has to be constantly innovated and enhanced in order for the brand to be successful rather than diluted.

9

SUSTAINABLE DEVELOPMENT IN THE LUXURY INDUSTRY: BEYOND THE APPARENT OXYMORON

Christophe Sempels

9.1 INTRODUCTION

Everything seems to oppose the concepts of luxury and sustainable development. French consumers, for example, evaluate the degree of association between luxury and sustainable development at the same level as they do for sustainable development and oil companies or banks.[1] This comes as no surprise if luxury is considered inessential, superfluous, exclusive and ostentatious, as these are the exact opposite of the values conveyed by sustainable development. So, is that the end of the story? Not if we add that luxury is also about craftsmanship and sense of *savoir-faire*, an example-setting industry associated with authenticity, high quality, durability and timelessness of models. By paraphrasing the philosopher Dominique Bourg, sustainable development is a question of rediscovering a lifestyle based on quality at the expense of quantity. This suggests that there is a clear bridge between luxury and sustainable development, especially when luxury brands have the power to influence consumer aspiration and behaviors.[2]

Many drivers should motivate luxury companies to engage in more sustainable business practices and these points will be developed further. Few companies however have taken the road of sustainability, the sector having a poor track record and being slow to engage.[3] The first part of this chapter will demonstrate that luxury brands are missing opportunities by not engaging in sustainability leadership. Then, practical ways to implement sustainable development in the business agenda of luxury companies will be addressed, both at strategic and operational levels.

9.2 SUSTAINABLE DEVELOPMENT: JUST A MATTER OF COMMON SENSE

Why should a company invest in sustainable development? This question may already have been answered by many companies, but additional insights may be needed for luxury companies. According to Graydon Carter, editor-in-chief of *Vanity Fair*, 'for the new generation, luxury brands that will not take environmental issues into consideration will lose most of their appeal. Modern brands must address these questions. Ignoring them would be old-fashioned and would equal a return to the previous century.' [4] It is often quoted that the first driver to engage in sustainability is the consumer, especially new generations of consumers, who are demanding more sustainability from the brands they purchase. But does the sustainable luxury consumer really exist?

9.3 THE SUSTAINABLE LUXURY CONSUMER

Market studies conducted worldwide have highlighted a rapid rise in the awareness of environmental issues among consumers. In the United States, the sociologist Paul H. Ray and the psychologist Sherry R. Anderson have identified a large segment of the adult population that lies beyond the classical sociological groups of modernists and traditionalists. The 'cultural creatives',[5] who account for 24 percent of the adult population (in other words, 50 million people), show strong awareness of planet-wide issues. They love nature, care about its preservation and call for more action and less talk. They question how big companies use their profits, especially how they destroy the environment and exploit poorer countries. In France, where the study was replicated in 2007, 17 percent of the adult population was classified as belonging to the group of cultural creatives.[6] In Europe, this represents more than 90 million people.

Studies have also shown that the group of cultural creatives is overrepresented by more educated people with higher socio-professional status. Importantly, cultural creatives dislike the representation of success of the modern materialistic culture. Success in their eyes is not related to consumption or making money and showing it ostentatiously. This is a clear shift that impacts the luxury industry, especially when some experts argue that in the west, more and more devoted luxury shoppers 'have been hiding their shopping bags' since September 2008.[7] Behavior that is confirmed by the owner of a caviar restaurant in Paris who explained that some of his clients were so painfully aware of the gap between the haves and the have-nots that they enter his restaurant through the less conspicuous staff entrance.[8]

High-end consumers seem to be changing their attitudes and are increasingly concerned about environmental issues.[9] All respondents from the 25 percent of better-off households know what sustainable development means and 98 percent are aware of the key related issues. Of the wealthiest, 47 percent claim they would accept to pay more for sustainable products (compared to 33 percent for the less well off).[10] Moreover, many wealthy consumers have been shocked by the financial crisis, many of them having lost money due to unethical and even illegal activities. Combined with a growing awareness of environmental issues, this has contributed to enhancing the social awareness of high-end consumers, many becoming truly socially conscious.[11] And compared to the baby boomer generation, the Gen X and Y, who wield the new spending power, are much more socially and environmentally aware.

While the rise of social and environmental consciousness is undisputable in Western countries, what about the rest of the world, especially in Asia, the booming continent for luxury markets? In January 2010, LOHAS Asia – (Lifestyles of Health and Sustainability), a market segment focused on health, the environment, personal development, sustainable living and social justice – partnered with the Natural Marketing Institute to conduct an online survey of more than 18,000 consumers across China, India, Singapore and seven other countries in Asia. Among the highlights revealed by the survey was a very real desire for sustainably made products in Asia, with Indonesia, China and India leading the way,[12] and a risk of boycott of over-packaged goods, for example. According to the Deeper Luxury Report from WWF, there is strong evidence that the urban middle classes across Asia, Latin America and Eastern Europe are being swept up by the eco-wave. In Asia, where there is a long tradition of ecological awareness from Taoism and Buddhism, green consumerism is growing by becoming a 'cool' phenomenon. In 2006, the customers of the Thai OSISU luxury recycled furniture company were 10 percent Asian and 90 percent Western, a year after it was 50:50.[13] In China, the most promising luxury market, a dramatic transformation is taking place in many mega cities as sustainable development government policies are implemented at a pace that far outstrips anything seen in the rest of the world. This is particularly true in Shanghai where the World Expo 2010 was organized under the flagship 'Better city, better life'.[14] Between 2006 and 2009, in preparation for the exposition, the Chinese government launched the China Environmental Awareness Program with the support of the UNDP, aiming to raise public awareness of the environmental challenges facing China and to convert that knowledge into attitudes, behaviors and practices toward environmental protection.

Awareness is also growing in Latin America and in the European Union's newest member states. The phenomenon is global, and a new trend is emerging throughout the world: environmental responsibility is conferring a new status on individuals.

Business-to-business customers seem to be following the same trend. The general manager of a famous Palace in Monaco reported that five years ago, when their B2B customers were negotiating rooms for organizing seminars, they did not ask any questions about the sustainable development policy of the hotel. Today, such questions are almost routine, especially for US customers. The 2008 IFOP survey on 401 top managers from big French companies[15] showed that the first stakeholders to be questioned about their sustainable development policy are their suppliers or service providers. Another study from IFOP[16] in 2009 revealed that 86 percent of the large companies (more than 5000 employees) are particularly demanding about the sustainable development policy of their suppliers, subcontractors or service providers.

9.4 WELCOME TO THE WORLD OF RARE RESOURCES

Beside the growing interest of consumers in more sustainable business practices, sustainable development should retain the attention of companies for a pragmatic concern, resource management. Every company has to rely on resources to manufacture its products or deliver its services. Resource management affects the competitiveness of companies, and is profoundly related to sustainable issues. The challenge for luxury businesses goes today far beyond the Washington Convention on International Trade in Endangered Species of Wild Fauna and Flora, which came into force on 1 July 1975 and has impacted many luxury businesses such as fashion (fur, skin), jewelry and table art (ivory) or cosmetics (flora). The various reports from national and international institutions on earth protection are unanimous: the pressure exerted by the Man on the planet is unsustainable. The Global Footprint Network Association has been raising the alarm for many years. By measuring what the Earth can regenerate and what man consumes to meet his various needs, the conclusion is compelling: our rate of consumption goes well beyond what the planet can renew in terms of resources. The association's most recent data show that it takes about one year and six months to generate the ecological services (production of resources and absorption of CO_2) that humanity requires in a year.[17] Many resources such as energy, water, arable land, fisheries, minerals, forest resources are already overexploited. Consistently optimistic in the past about future energy supplies, the International Energy Agency proclaimed that conventional crude supplies most likely peaked in 2006, and that unconventional supplies, which are already more expensive to exploit, should peak in the next two decades.[18] Conventional gas should peak in less than 15 years, and coal in the mid-twenty-first century.[19] When we know that 80 percent of global energy consumption is based on fossil fuels, we can expect a structural pressure on energy prices in the following years. By extension, this will affect the cost structure of many luxury companies in the hotel, tourism, airlines or yachting industries.

The same holds for gold, a key resource for some luxury players. Gold demand is subdivided into central bank reserve increases, jewelry production, industrial consumption and investment. Aaron

Regent, president of the Canadian gold giant Barrick Gold, claimed at the end of 2009 that 'there is a strong case to be made that we are already at "peak gold". Production peaked around 2000 and it has been in decline ever since, and we forecast that decline to continue. It is increasingly difficult to find ore.'[20] In the same way, iron, copper, bauxite and chromite, among others, are considered by the Chinese government as insufficiently available, both in quantity and in quality to fuel Chinese growth alone.[21] Imagine then the result when we add the rest of the world.

Entering into the world of rare resources means that we are entering into the world of expensive resources, as the French Economic and Social Council to French companies states. Being more resource efficient is therefore not only good for the planet, but also rational to lighten the cost structure of companies. You may feel it is not new, and indeed it is not. The Club of Rome published *Limits to Growth* in 1972 arguing that we were rapidly running out of essential resources and offering solutions related to using resources more efficiently. In 1998, they were more concrete by publishing *Factor Four: Doubling Wealth, Halving Resource Use* where they called for reaching the factor 4, meaning that resource productivity could and should grow fourfold. Thirteen years later, the message has still not been heard, and the pressure on resources is increasing. The fashion industry (as distinct from the luxury industry) is particularly concerned about the shorter life cycle of many products due to fast fashion trends.

More sustainable resource management should therefore be a quest for all luxury companies for several reasons: to gain efficiency, to foster innovation with the development of advanced technologies (such as Tesla – the premium electric car), to lighten the cost structure, to secure a sustainable supply of raw material that could enhance brand reputation and trust and that could reduce the environmental impact of the company.

9.5 SUSTAINABLE DEVELOPMENT, A MUST IN TERMS OF REPUTATION MANAGEMENT

Resources are not only an environmental issue. The social conditions of their extraction and exploitation are crucial for luxury companies for whom reputation is a core intangible asset. Luxury brands are indeed more sensitive to reputational damage, because a greater proportion of their brand value is derived from empathy and trust.[22] Sourcing is clearly under pressure and NGO's, Internet and the film industry do not hesitate to denounce unethical practices. The movie *Dirty Paradise*, winner of the *Grand Prix 2010* at the Human Rights Film Festival in Geneva, broadcasts the story of a thousand Indians who are trying to survive the devastation caused by 10,000 illegal gold-seekers who hide in the forests. Greenpeace has also often condemned mining practices for gold and other precious metals and their negative impact on the displacement of communities, contamination of drinking water and fish kills, destruction of virgin environment or poor working conditions and utilization of toxic substances in the extraction processes.[23] Through the Internet, scandals now have a worldwide audience, such as the recent suspicion of a local government in Philippines and large-scale mining companies that could have been involved in the killing of a broadcast journalist and environmentalist actively involved in preserving the biodiversity and environment of the area against large-scale and foreign mining.[24] The success of the movie *Blood Diamond*, showing how diamonds are mined in African war zones and sold to finance conflicts, has raised concern about the ethics behind the diamond business. Despite the reactions of De Beers, arguing that the trade in conflict diamonds had been reduced from 4 percent to 1 percent of total purchases, the image of this noble material has been flawed.

While the sourcing is under pressure, the raw materials themselves are under the scrutiny of public opinion and associations. The Peta Association – People for the Ethical Treatment of Animals – has for many years led particularly strong global campaigns against fur. Many celebrities have decided to collaborate with the famous 'Rather go naked than wear fur' campaign.[25] Peta has also put particularly intense pressure on some designers such as Donna Karan, with shocking websites like dkbunnybutcher.com or fashion shows that were ruined by Peta's fur protest.

What may have a tremendous impact on consumers may also force celebrities to disengage from their endorsement. WWF has called celebrities not to support brands with poor social and environmental performance. The emergence of ecorazzi – paparazzi that track celebrities and notables in support of the environment and humanitarian causes and that do not hesitate to point out inconsistency between their words and deeds – and the success of their websites[26] clearly encourage celebrities to check that the brands they support do not damage their own reputation.

The social dimension of sustainable development clearly challenges the reputation of luxury industry as a whole, especially in a society where inequalities are growing. For example, when announcing in December 2009 the future opening of the Royal Monceau super-deluxe hotel in Paris, BBC News ran the headline 'Parisian luxury hotels mask city's growing poverty'. With the geographical broadening of the luxury industry in markets with huge inequalities and significant poverty such as China or India, this is more relevant than ever. We have already discussed the consumer trends to avoid conspicuous consumption. The Deeper Luxury report pointed out the concern of governments – such as Indian, Chinese or Egyptian – questioning the social acceptability of luxury in societies with high inequality. In some cases, drastic solutions were imposed, such as in Beijing where the mayor ordered all luxury billboards to be removed from the capital. How luxury can contribute to the shaping of a harmonious society is clearly a question that should not be eluded by companies, not only because it can serve or deserve their reputation, but also because not taking this into account would probably increase restrictions and actions such as that of Beijing's mayor.

Luxury is about excellence, it is about authenticity, values and quality. When people's set of values is enriched by pro-environmental and pro-social considerations, it targets the essence of luxury. In the same way, quality is no longer a matter of intrinsic quality of products alone. Quality is broader and now relates not only to what is produced, but also to how it has been produced[27] and how it is delivered to the customers through relational quality and outstanding experience. As Jean-Noël Kapferer stated, 'luxury brands must create their identities not only by the name, personality, and style of the founder, but also through values by which they should be known and publicly judged'. Sustainable development offers a particularly suitable platform to enrich the value-set of the brand.

The list of drivers that encourage luxury companies to engage more seriously in sustainable development is still long and a whole book could be written on them. The DNA of luxury brands and the two key assets of companies – consumers and reputation – are clearly affected by sustainability. Ignoring sustainable development or considering it as a minor issue is now becoming a clear managerial mistake.

9.6 CREATING VALUE THROUGH SUSTAINABLE DEVELOPMENT

Being convinced that sustainable development is now a must for luxury companies is not enough to create both financial and non-financial value through its integration into the business agenda. Here we will present the key dimensions of this integration.

9.6.1 Revisiting the strategy in the light of sustainable development

To be credible, a sustainable strategy must first be embodied in the company's core business, not simply in its peripheral activities. Stakeholders' expectations clearly focus on the activities where the impact is the highest. These are always in the core business. A champagne producer may decide to recycle its paper, but the key impact is in the grape vine, in the bottling and in the logistic process. Value may therefore be generated from sustainable development only if strategy is revisited. But the process of this strategy review should also be adapted. The classical strategic elaboration process is a 'closed' process. It is the mission of the corporate to define the corporate strategy, the strategic business units being in charge of the definition of the competitive strategies and their implementation. The strategy is designed by the company members, sometimes helped by consultants.

But knowledge increasingly lies outside the organization, especially in the complex field of sustainable development. The first key difference when revisiting the strategy to integrate sustainable development is thus to open the process to stakeholders. The ability of a company to meet the expectations of a larger panel of stakeholders – not only the well-known or salient ones, but also those with opposing views – may indeed generate numerous benefits. It fosters innovation, improves the efficiency of a company, and induces a better acceptance of the company's activities. By integrating stakeholders into the strategy development process, it reduces misunderstandings by fostering dialogue. At a time where knowledge is a key driver of competitive advantage, it helps to build imagination, extends the knowledge of the impact of activities and integrates asymmetric resources and new capabilities to find solutions to complex challenges posed by sustainable development. At the end of the process, disruptive new business strategies may emerge and their credibility is enhanced. And, despite the effort of a company to manage risk, collaborating with the stakeholders may help companies to anticipate and prevent crises or to facilitate the management of a crisis, thanks to known contacts, established relationships based on trust and so on.[28]

Integrating stakeholders allows the mapping of all the tensions from their various expectations. In short, shareholders want to maximize financial return; employees want better working conditions, a stimulating working environment and good wages; NGOs call for a reduction in the environmental impacts of the activities and a generation of positive social externalities; authorities expect compliance with regulations, stability of the economic activities and employment in their area. These generic formulations must of course be fine-tuned to the particular activities of the companies. A jewelry company, for example, will see its sourcing of precious material under pressure, while carbon emission will be a key issue for a high-end airline or a private jet company. Looking for solutions to manage these tensions in an acceptable way for every stakeholder usually results in the design of a disruptive strategy that may foster the competitiveness of companies or create new market spaces.

Managing the participation of stakeholders in the strategy development process is not an easy task. Many barriers exist to prevent the successful collaboration of multiple partners showing many asymmetries, such as misunderstanding or mistrust between the actors, the gap between the actions of NGOs and those of companies, the lack of opportunities to meet and to become acquainted, the difficulties to grasp the motivation to commit to such partnership and to identify valuable sources of expertise and the difficulties to manage such interactions.[29] The success of such integrations depends on the following key factors:

- Selection of credible and legitimate partners, with the motivations of each participant, their key resources and expectations to create a win-win climate clearly detailed
- Formalization of a precise and flexible contractual framework that defines the rules of the game, the roles and the nature of their commitments, clear and realistic objectives, the resources and capabilities that will be shared and the way they will be shared to enhance trust
- Investment in transparent and clear communication
- Strong managerial involvement and commitment from the top, and from people in charge of the partnership
- Regular evaluation of the partnership progress and a clear definition of indicators of performance of the alliance
- Capitalization plus a strong management of the 'alliances management knowledge', the barriers and key success factors of the partnership.[30]

9.6.2 Revisiting products, services and processes for more eco-efficiency

'To break the around the world record, you need to be fast. And to be fast, you need to be light. You take with you the minimum of resources.'[31] Helen MacArthur, the famous sailor, who has founded an independent charity to inspire people to re-think, re-design and build a sustainable future, conveys here a powerful idea: performance is related to the way you manage your resources.

Beside strategy, the core business activities of any companies are made up of products and services, and are structured by processes. Making them more eco-efficient may allow companies to generate competitive edges that are either external (e.g. preference from consumers, positive impact on reputation, ability to charge a higher premium price) or internal (cost reduction or efficiency gains).

According to the World Business Council for Sustainable Development, eco-efficiency refers to the delivery of 'competitively priced goods and services that satisfy human needs and bring quality of life while progressively reducing environmental impacts of goods and resource intensity throughout the entire life-cycle to a level at least in line with the Earth's estimated carrying capacity'.[32] The critical dimensions of eco-efficiency are:[33]

■ A reduction in the material intensity of goods or services
■ A reduction in the energy intensity of goods or services
■ Reduced dispersion of toxic materials
■ Improved recyclability
■ Maximum use of renewable resources
■ Greater durability of products
■ Increased service intensity of goods and services

9.6.3 Life cycle analysis and eco-design

Several management methods have been developed to support eco-efficiency efforts within organizations. The life cycle analysis (LCA) aims to compile and analyze energy consumption, the use of raw materials and emissions into the environment. It assesses the potential impact of a product, a service or a process on the environment throughout its whole life cycle, from extraction of raw materials to the management of the product at the end of its life. Its application is structured by 14040 and related ISO standards that specify the principles and framework of life cycle analysis. In support of the life cycle analysis, eco-design is a holistic approach that integrates environmental considerations in the design or redesign of products or services along their whole life cycle, while maintaining their quality of use. It is internationally standardized in ISO 14062.

LVMH is an example of a luxury group that has decided to invest in eco-innovation and eco-design not only because it is good for the planet, but also because it is good for the business. The road is still long, but programs have been launched in every business unit, the focus depending on the key issues of each activity. They include the reduction of packaging weight and volume, the choice of components and raw materials, the use of more energy and water-efficient production processes, and initiatives to comply with the Reach regulations.[34] With eco-efficiency, small changes may have large effects. By reducing the corrugated inserts in the packaging of Christian Dior, Kenzo, Givenchy and Guerlain perfumes from $90g/m^2$ to $80g/m^2$, the use of cardboard has been reduced by 186 tons without losing any esthetic qualities. The Hennessy Fine Cognac H2O has been also eco-redesigned.

> The weight of the glass has been reduced from 780g to 600g; the glass was labeled in enamels without ink or glue or paper, the cork is now made of beech wood from FSC certified forests, the box is also FSC certified and bleached without chlorine with printed product information on the inside, shipping cartons are lighter because they are simply fluted and have only the legal notices on them so as to limit ink use.

In their five business units, the weights of the packaging in metric tons was reduced globally by 20 percent between 2008 and 2009.[35] (By 22 percent for Wines and Spirits, 10 percent for Fashion and Leather Goods, 13 percent for Perfumes and Cosmetics, 8 percent for Watches and Jewelry, and 14 percent for selective retailing.)

The benefits of eco-design and life cycle analysis are numerous. Less expensive resources means a lighter cost structure. Less weight results in a reduction of transport costs and lower gas emissions. Fewer toxic substances equal more safety for consumers and employees. After eco-redesigning their products, some companies were able to profitably relocate activities from Asia to their home country. Compliance with existing and upcoming regulations (such as Reach) is improved. The generated competitive advantages are not only internal, but may add extra value externally. The ability to differentiate the brand is broader because stories may be told about the whole life cycle of the product, and not only on its usage stage (the positive externalities in the country of extraction of raw material or a specific agro-technique in a grape vine that could strengthen the experience of the consumers with the brand). As discussed, the value-set of the brand may be nurtured

172

by pro-environmental or pro-social actions of the company that in turn increase the brand appeal.

9.6.4 Imitate the nature: A new mindset to innovate

'We must draw our standards from the natural world. We must honor them with the humility of the wise, the bounds of that natural world, and the mystery which lies beyond them, admitting that there is something in the order of being which evidently exceeds all our competence.' With this quote, Vaclav Havel, the former President of the Czech Republic, inspired the emergence of a new discipline based on the intelligence of the nature. Biomimicry is the science and art of emulating nature's best biological ideas and then imitating these designs and processes to solve human problems.[36] The swimwear manufacturer Speedo has, for example, developed a full body swimsuit inspired by the way a shark's skin reduces friction and channels the water over the body as the shark moves.[37] The 3 percent improvement in swimming speed due to this 'shark-skin' suit likely contributed to the fact that 80 percent of the swimming medals won in the 2000 Olympics were won by athletes wearing Speedo suits; swimmers wearing the suit also broke 13 of 15 world records.[38] A better understanding of the structure of shark skin has many applications, such as friction reduction or auto-cleaning parasites from their surface (with potential benefits in terms of innovation for yachting, cars, aircraft for surface coating and new material development among others).

Nature gives us many lessons.[39] First, nature uses solar as its primary source of energy and it uses only what it needs to operate. It seeks to optimize rather than maximize and focus on designing better systems rather than better components. In terms of design, the form is adapted to the usage or the problem that needs to be solved. Nature recycles everything, produced wastes being considered as resources that are valorized (when a tree loses its leaves, they fall to its base, decompose and become biological nutrients captured by roots to feed the tree). Nature banks on cooperation and diversity. It relies on local competences and capabilities, and uses constraints as a source of innovation and adaptation.

The Biomimicry Institute provides a valuable framework to use biomimicry as a tool for innovation.[40] This is a six-step process:

(1) Identification and specification of the problem that needs to be solved (specification of the functions that need to be accomplished, the people who are involved both with the problem and the possible implementation of its solution and the location of the problem)
(2) Interpretation, which means biologizing the question by translating the design brief set up in the previous stage from nature's perspective (the basic idea is to analyze how nature does this function)
(3) Discovery of the champions in nature who answer or solve the problem
(4) Abstraction by identifying and analyzing the repeating patterns and processes within nature that achieve success
(5) Emulation so that ideas and solutions based on the natural models may be implemented (mimicking being achieved on form, function and (eco)system)
(6) Evaluation of the effectiveness of the implemented solution and comparison with the solution implemented by nature.

Biomimicry is particularly relevant to the redesigning of products or processes in order to make them more sustainable, sustainability being at the root of nature's functioning. It is moreover particularly relevant for luxury brands while design, authenticity and originality are key strategic resources. And what could be more authentic than the intelligence of Nature. Just look at the futuristic project of 'Mangal City' to understand it practically. This project is a series of futuristic spiraling skyscrapers designed by the Chimera team for London. It has been inspired by the complex ecosystems created by the mangrove tree, defining an urban ecosystem while supporting housing and cultural programs. The new office for the Ministry of Municipality Affairs & Agriculture in Qatar – designed as a giant cactus – is another beautiful example of luxury house design based on biomimicry.

Recycling is particularly interesting and should be considered in its broader sense, for both product or service design and process reengineering. Whirlpool for example is ready to launch the

Green Kitchen,[41] a vanguard kitchen where all the appliances are eco-efficient and interconnected as an ecosystem. The refrigerator is equipped with a tray that prevents cold air from escaping when the door opens, allowing an energy saving of 50 percent. Energy-efficient appliances can self-regulate for energy savings (auto-regulation, nature takes only what is required to function). The smoke and the steam produced during cooking are detected so that the hood automatically regulates the aspiration power and the light (optimize rather than maximize). The vitroceramic plates adjust the heating area to the size of the pan, while the oven self-regulates the temperature by automatically detecting the type of dish. Inspired by natural cycles, the kitchen interconnects all the appliances in order to reduce and/or recycle the water, heat and energy of the whole system (waste being considered a resource). The heat produced in the compressor coils of the fridge, for instance, is used to heat the water of the dishwasher. Clean cold tap water is automatically detected and diverted into a special tank to be reused. In total, 60 percent of the water and heat generated from the kitchen are diverted to fuel other appliances. All these innovations allow a reduction in total cost of energy bills by 70 percent.

These advantages provide the key argument for the commercial launch of this kitchen in 2012. The Green Kitchen was also honored with the coveted iF Product Design Award 2009 delivered by the prestigious International Forum Design, a global benchmark in design. The same holds for processes. What are the extrants you should consider as a valuable resource rather than just a waste. Every company has, for example, computer server rooms. The heat generated by servers is neutralized by energy-consuming air-conditioning. At the same time, heat is needed to warm the offices and it is produced by energy-consuming radiators. This simplistic example highlights what we could gain by considering this situation, and many others, as a system rather than a series of isolated components. Applications of such principles may foster the imagination and enrich the innovation capabilities of many luxury companies from many sectors. A famous Palace located in Nice, France, has decided to use this principle to increase its environmental performance, the swimming pool being, for example, heated by the unused calories recuperated from several appliances of the hotel. Based on this logic, the sky is the limit.

9.7 SUSTAINABLE SERVICE SYSTEMS TO DECOUPLE WEALTH GENERATION FROM RESOURCES AND ENERGY USE

At a time of rarefaction of resources, doing more with less should become a keyword. Eco-efficient and biomimicry bring important potential savings in terms of resources and energy savings. A much more promising innovative approach to get significant results in terms of decoupling is to shift the business focus from designing and selling goods to delivering sustainable service systems that supply the same service as the good by providing a usage function or a global need-fulfillment solution to customers.[42] For example, rather than selling lamps or heating (goods), 'light comfort' or 'thermal comfort' may be proposed to customers (a global need-fulfillment system coupled with environmental benefits if properly designed). Shifting from products to services may be particularly interesting for luxury companies at a time when conspicuous consumption is called into question, when specialists consider we are entering in a form of post-materialism period with an emphasis on experience (at least in Western countries)[43] and when luxury consumers are seeking service values that could create and consistently deliver these extraordinary experiences.[44] Moreover, the associated hassles of owning a product may be eliminated with this shift, for more convenience for the consumers. (This question however needs deeper investigation as ownership is also a source of value in itself, especially in the Western countries.)

Two configurations of sustainable service systems may be distinguished: the usage-oriented services and the result-oriented services. With usage-oriented services, the good (1) is made available in a different form to the consumer, (2) is sometimes shared by a number of users, (3) stays in the ownership of the provider. It is the usage of the good (i.e. a service) rather than the good itself that is invoiced, without transfer of ownership. The potential environmental benefit results from the ability of the provider to deliver the service in a systemic mindset, where eco-efficiency and closed-loop flow of resources are integrated.

This approach is primarily used today in the B2B context, such as Rolls Royce Aerospace that no longer simply sells aero engines, but offers a total care package where customers buy the capability the engine delivers, that is the 'power by the hour'. Rolls-Royce retains responsibility for risk and maintenance, generating revenues by making the engine available for use.[45] This kind of business approach allows the company to implement more easily the 3R approach: Reduce – Reuse – Recycle. *Reduce* refers to eco-efficiency and calls for minimizing the use of natural resources and energy in developing products, services and processes, for the same service rendered. *Reuse* aims to maximize the lifetime of the product either by an extension of its life or by judicious replacement of some components only, so that a maximum of materials can be preserved as long as possible (this is perfectly in line with the durability and timelessness of models characterizing the luxury industry). Finally, *Recycle* redirects a maximum of materials contained in products at the end of life into new productive cycles rather than transforming them into invaluable wastes.

This approach should be particularly relevant for products or facilities that are used quite infrequently by luxury consumers. They could still benefit from the usage of exclusive products while not having to support the hassles of managing them the whole year. This also offers variety and flexibility to change the model as often as desired, such as Bag Borrow or Steal that offers women an exciting new means of enjoying the luxury accessories they love. Members have access to over 3000 styles of authentic luxury handbags and jewelry, including accessories, from renowned designers, with the flexibility to borrow by the week or month.[46]

The second kind of sustainable service system is the result-oriented services. In this most accomplished form of service system, the seller no longer sells a good to the customer but sells the desired result rendered by the good. Rather than selling energy as a volume of kw/h, the basic idea is to sell the service rendered by energy, for example, provide consumers with thermal comfort. The price of the service being now based on a service level agreement (SLA), energy becomes an input – that is, a cost – that should be minimized to reach the SLA. And the consumer is sure to get the negotiated level of service, any failure being automatically and quickly solved by the provider to avoid the contractually defined penalties. The focus is thus on experience and not on products that are just considered as a vehicle to deliver the service.

These result-oriented services could be implemented in many contexts: smart homes with security management contract, body care or healthcare, leisure and so on. You may argue that those services already exist and that they are not innovative. This may be true, but not, however, in this configuration, when a systemic approach is conducted and the optimization of the system is sought in order to deliver the service level agreement in the most efficient way. A smart home should allow energy consumption to be managed in an integrated systemic approach, based on the special needs and the presence of the occupants. In addition, security systems may be integrated into the smart system, for more convenience and safety for the occupants. A system to improve the well-being and the healthcare of people may be developed, by integrating several component such as (1) a smart luxury watch that could measure and send in real-time data such as blood pressure, heart beat, physical exercises, hours and quality of sleep, (2) smart scales that measure the weight, the blood pressure and the adipose (fat) rate, (3) a diagnostic center with well-being, sport, beauty, nutrition and healthcare experts that collect and analyze the data and provide personalized program, (4) a network of partners such as sports center, beauty center, restaurant, where the consumer may implement his/her personalized program[47] .... All these components already exist, but the innovation is to integrate these resources into a system designed to render an outstanding and complete service to the consumers. The social benefit is clear in terms of positive impact on health. Environmental gains could result from a better diet (appropriate quantity of food, less meat – producing meat is highly carbon emitting – and more vegetables, organic being preferred and encouraged). They could also result from the pooling of sport or beauty equipment, for example, that is no longer purchased by the consumers but used in the partners' exclusive centers. The same idea of system innovation may be applied to leisure, mobility and so on.

9.8 DELIVER SOCIAL ADDED VALUE

As discussed earlier, the rise of inequalities all around the world and the socioeconomic situation of many countries such as India or China are exerting pressure on the dimensions of exclusivity and elitism attached to the luxury industry. Contributing to the delivery of social added value in countries where a luxury brand operates would undoubtedly increase the brand reputation and equity, both for more concerned consumers and for authorities that regulate these markets.

Many luxury companies support foundations or charity projects, some having set up their own foundation. Hermès for example created the *Fondation d'entreprise Hermès*[48] in 2008. The supported projects are structured around four areas closely related with the core values of Hermès: (1) the promotion of traditional craft skills; (2) support for the creative arts; (3) commitment to education and training to help children in countries with poor or no access to education to acquire the personal and professional skills they need to lead independent lives; and (4) environmental concerns.

While there is little doubt that setting up a foundation is useful, particularly if it is related to the core values of companies, there is still a separation between the business and the social activities. Some companies have decided to close the gap by supporting a social cause directly through their business activities. Toms Shoes for example gives a pair of new shoes to a child in need for each pair of shoes or shirt a consumer purchases. Toms' claim is simple and punchy: one for one. The company Jacinto & Lirio creates fashionable items out of water hyacinth. In spite of its seemingly innocent exterior, this flower is in fact a pernicious and invasive species that dramatically impacts water flow, blocks sunlight from reaching native aquatic plants and starves the water of oxygen, often killing fish or turtles. The plants also create a prime habitat for mosquitoes, the classic vectors of disease.[49] The social impact of this flower is devastating. By purchasing a Jacinto & Lirio (J&L) product, consumers help to fight against the spread of water hyacinth, but also to empower the local community in Pampanga, Philippines, with whom J&L collaborates.

Gucci decided in 2005 to participate in a global partnership with UNICEF. In the six-year period from 2005 to 2010, Gucci committed over $9 million to UNICEF, making Gucci the largest corporate donor to UNICEF's 'Schools for Africa' initiative.[50] More interestingly, Frida Giannini, the Creative Director of Gucci, decided in 2007 to create a special product to extend the company's

SUSTAINABLE DEVELOPMENT IN THE LUXURY INDUSTRY

commitment to UNICEF throughout the year. The first exclusive 'Gucci for UNICEF' bag was launched in November 2007 and was dedicated to UNICEF for one full year to increase its fundraising potential. Since then, Gucci has continued this tradition by developing every year an annual product to enhance the partnership.

Even though it is not a pure luxury brand, Ben & Jerry's (B&J), the premium ice-cream brand, is an inspiring example of how the core business can be linked to social added value. It has decided to source its cookies from the Greyston Bakery in New York that seeks to train and counsel the homeless by hiring only hard-to-employ people. When the bakery was close to bankruptcy, it asked B&J's foundation for financial support. Rather than provide money, B&J's decided to give them a much more valuable asset for the future: an exclusive contract to supply the company with cookies for its chocolate fudge brownie ice cream, which is now one of the top-selling flavors worldwide. At the beginning, B&J's helped Greyston to develop reliable and qualitative production process to be able to honor the contract properly. Being a social for-profit enterprise, all profits from Greyston Bakery are channeled to the Greyston Foundation, where they are used on behalf of the local community. This example is a perfect illustration of the powerful social impact a company may have when it decides to use its core activity as a source of social added value for the local community in which it operates. As explained above, it is only when the strategy and the core business of the company are called into question that a real social or environmental impact may be made.

9.9 CONCLUSION

Luxury and sustainable development are not always easy to connect, the two being full of prejudices. In this chapter, we have tried to demonstrate that connections are much more natural than they may seem at first sight. First, more and more luxury consumers expect their brands to commit to a sustainable approach. Then, compared to other industries, it may be easier for luxury brands to engage in sustainable development due to inherent differences in their business model. As discussed, the luxury industry is committed to quality, focusing on quality rather than quantity, and usually uses less energy-intensive production methods and produces in countries with higher labor standards. The DNA of the luxury industry and the values of quality, durability, timelessness of models, authenticity or *savoir-faire* are in line with sustainable development. And while the price premium charged for sustainable products is often a barrier to purchase in mass markets, it is clearly not an issue for luxury brands that deliver strong value, the high margins allowing companies to change existing methods.

Despite this convergence, both experts and NGOs conclude that luxury companies should engage more deeply in sustainable development, despite the effort conducted by some of them. It is not only moral sense, but just common sense and a demonstration of strong managerial competences. This however calls for new managerial skills and new knowledge, most often located outside the company.

In order to create both financial and non-financial value by integrating sustainable development, there is at least one must: it must be incorporated in the core strategy of the company, in its core business. Revisiting strategy is therefore the first step to sustainable development, and it requires the involvement of the top executive level. Once this is achieved, revisiting the core products and services and the underlying processes to make them more eco-efficient and/or more socially responsible becomes natural, and allows the generation of both internal and external competitive advantage while fostering imagination, innovation and the creation of new strategic spaces.

Of course, much more could and should be said about sustainable development in the luxury industry. This single chapter could be easily transformed into a whole book. Many other key questions still need to be addressed, such as counterfeiting, employees' expectations to attract and retain the best talents, evaluating, reporting and communicating the sustainability efforts. The regulatory point of view needs to be developed, as does managing eco-innovation, innovating on business models or activities to deliver social benefits or to significantly decouple the generation of wealth from the use of resources and energy. The key role of the luxury industry is to set up trends and to influence consumers beyond the targeted luxury markets. Clearly, the story is only just beginning.

NOTES

CHAPTER 1

* The following sources have been used in this chapter: Grant, J. (2006), *The Brand Innovation Manifesto: How to Build Brands, Redefine Markets and Defy Conventions*, Chichester, England: John Wiley & Sons; Smith, C. (2010), *Dreaming of Dior: Every Dress Tells a Story*, New York: Atria Books; Karbo, K. and Chanel, C. (2009), *The Gospel According to Coco Chanel: Life Lessons from the World's Most Elegant Woman*, Guilford, Conn: Skirt!; Groom, N. S. J. (1997), *The New Perfume Handbook*, London: Blackie Academic & Professional; Steele, V. (1991), *Women of Fashion: Twentieth-century Designers*, New York: Rizzoli International; Zaleznik, A. (1993), *Learning Leadership: Cases and Commentaries on Abuses of Power in Organizations*, Chicago, IL: Bonus Books; Okonkwo, U. (2007), *Luxury Fashion Branding: Trends, Tactics, Techniques*, Basingstoke: Palgrave Macmillan; Gidel, H. (2008), *Coco Chanel*, Praha: Garamond; www.lvmh.com; Haig, M. (2006), *Brand Royalty: How the World's Top 100 Brands Thrive & Survive*, London: Kogan Page; Luxury in Emerging Markets, Separating facts from fiction, *Luxury in Asia Conference,* Paris; Unity Marketing's Luxury Report (2006), *Overview Luxury Market Study*; Securities, N. (2008), La richesse des pays émergents, *Etude sectorielle.*

1 Jollant-Kneebone, F. and Braunstein, C. (2003), *Atelier A – Rencontre de l'Art et de l'Objet*, Paris, Norma Éditions.

2 France Economic and Social Council (Conseil Economique et Social) (2008), Text presented by Mme Jacqueline Socquet-Clerc Lafont, Le Luxe: Production et Services.

3 Silverstein, M. and Fiske, N. (2003), *Trading Up: The New American Luxury*, New York, Portfolio Hardcover, p. 336.

4 Hanna, J. (2004), Luxury Isn't What It Used to Be, *Harvard Business School Working Knowledge*, published 16 August 2004, source: http://hbswk.hbs.edu/item/4321.html, retrieved 10 April 2011.

5 Okonkwo, U. (2009), 'The luxury brand strategy challenge', *Journal of Brand Management,* 16, 287–289.

6 Doctor Ravi Shanker is the Chairperson and Professor at the Indian Institute of Foreign Trade, New Delhi, India. He has authored five books and academic papers on Services Marketing.

7 http://neemranahotels.com/content/history-and-philosophy.

CHAPTER 2

1 Figures refer to financial years 2008/2009.

2 The profile detailed is the typical corresponds to the vast majority of luxury business actors, with the remarkable exception of the giants such as LVMH, PPR, Richemont.

3 Incoterms: International Commercial Terms used in international commercial transactions. Accepted by governments, companies and practitioners, for the interpretation of conditions applying to international trade.

4 For an easy and self-explanatory comparison, it can be noted that a distribution chain active in a single domestic market may generate a comparable turnover – 300 million – by operating only a dozen hypermarkets within a few tens of kilometers in the same region.

5 Figures and information on companies has been retrieved on public available sources and internet.

CHAPTER 3

1 Actual results may vary.

2 CFO stands for Chief Financial Officer who is the boss of the Finance function in a company.

3 To maximize value creation, everybody in a company should behave as if he or she were the owner. It is the actual owners' responsibility to align employees' incentives to theirs so that this really happens.

4 In fact, if a company goes bankrupt the assets are sold and the debt holders are paid first. What is left, if anything, goes then to the shareholders (owners).

5 This is not a precise definition, but since we are company owners and not accountants it is good enough.

6 We are valuing the inventory at sales value here, but it is often valued at production cost instead.

7 Actual results may vary.

8 In reality, a part of the money in a company's bank account is also considered working capital since you need at least liquidity to operate. Some types of short-term debt like bank overdraft accounts can also be considered working capital.

9 The State could also go bankrupt, so the risk is never zero in reality.

10 Unless you are a government-owned company at least.

11 In reality, you always have some recurring maintenance capital to keep things running.

12 There are different methods to model cash flows for valuation; we use here the Equity Cash Flows method. In academic books you can learn different valuation methods that are claimed to be *theoretically* more appropriate. In practice this is the one that works best.

13 The growth rate is another important aspect of determining a multiple. Fast growing companies get sold at a higher multiple than slow-growing ones.

14 You can actually find precise formulae in academic books to calculate discount rates which seem to make sense *theoretically* but are close to useless in practice.

15 You cannot calculate the IRR by hand, you will need a calculator to do it.

CHAPTER 4

1 We use the term product to refer both to a good and to a service. This chapter focuses mainly on goods rather than services, but

examples related to services will be given throughout the chapter. As a whole, we understand that what is delivered to a luxury client is a *service* in the sense of Vargo, Stephen and Lusch, Robert (2004), 'Evolving to a New Dominant Logic for Marketing', *Journal of Marketing*, vol. 68, January 2004, pp. 1–17.

2   Berry, C.J. (1994), *The Idea of Luxury: A Conceptual and Historical Investigation.* Cambridge: Cambridge University Press.

3   Kapferer, J.-N. and Bastien, V. (2009), *The Luxury Strategy: Break The Rules of Marketing to Build Strong Brands.* London & Philadelphia: Kogan Page Ltd.

4   Source: Documentaire Passion patrimoine : du Lot-et-Garonne à la Corrèze de Marie Maurice et Franck Dhelens, émission Des racines et des ailes, reportage sur l'abbaye d'Aubazine, 13 avril 2011 *in* http://fr.wikipedia.org/wiki/Coco_Chanel retrieved 27 April 2011.

5   Source: http://en.wikipedia.org/wiki/Coco_Chanel retrieved 27 April 2011.

6   Source:http://www.fashionmodeldirectory.com/designers/louis-vuitton/ retrieved 28 May 2011.

7   Source: http://fr.wikipedia.org/wiki/Route_de_la_soie retrieved 27 April 2011.

8   Kay, John (2004), *The Truth about Markets: Why Some Countries are Rich and Others Remains Poor.* London: Penguin.

9   Source: http://www.worldofluxuryus.com/watches/Richard-Mille/356.php retrieved 27 April 2011.

10 Richard Mille (2011), History, www.richardmille.com retrieved 15 May 2011.

11 De Bono, Edward (1967), *The Use of Lateral Thinking.* London: Cape.

12 This paragraph is adapted from http://fr.wikipedia.org/wiki/Karl_Lagerfeld retrieved 27 April 2011.

13 Source: « L'empereur des Jeux » documentary by Jean-Marie Hosatte and Philippe Bigot exhibited by France 5 on 24 April 2011.

14 Richard Mille (2011), History, www.richardmille.com retrieved 15 May 2011.

15 Verganti, R. (2008), 'Design, Meanings and Radical Innovation: A Meta-model and a Research Agenda', *Journal of Product Innovation Management*, vol. 25, 5, pp. 436–456.

16 Holbrook, M. (1999), *Consumer Value: A Framework for Analysis and Research.* London: Routledge.

17 Kim, W. C. and Mauborgne, R. (2005), *Blue Ocean Strategy.* Boston, MA: Harvard Business School Press.

18 Source: http://www.brainyquote.com/quotes/authors/a/andy_warhol.html#ixzz1NGHDLc3J retrieved 25 April 2011.

19 Kapferer, J.-N. and Bastien,V. (2009), op. cit.

20 World of Luxury (2011), Richard Mille, source: http://www.worldofluxuryus.com/watches/Richard-Mille/356.php retrieved 12 May 2011.

21 Richard Mille (2011), Philosophy, op. cit.

22 A more detailed account of the creation process can be found in Chapter 7, Managing Creation, of Chevalier, M. and Mazzalovo, G. (2008), *Luxury Brand Management.* Singapore: John Wiley&Sons (Asia) Pte. Ltd.

23 For a detailed discussion of that, refer to Chapter 8, Qualifying a product as luxury, of Kapferer, J-.N. and Bastien, V. (2009), op. cit.

24 The French Ministry of Culture created in 1994, the title of 'Maître d'Art' to recognize exceptional professionals in the art craftsmen. For example, the 2006 batch includes artisans from Hermès, Louis Vuitton, Chanel and Baccarat, whereas the 2008 batch rewarded artisans from Cartier, Christian Dior and the Sevres manufacture. Source: Comité Colbert, Maîtres d'Art : nos Trésors Vivants, retrieved from www.comitecolbert, on 12 May 2011.

25 Source: Interview de Francis Chauveau, Président Directeur Général de Saint-Louis,Président de la Commission Métiers et Ressources Humaines du Comité Colbert, 2005.

26 Kapferer, J-.N. and Bastien, V. (2009), op. cit., p. 158.

27 Chevalier, M. and Mazzalovo, G. (2008), op. cit.

28 Felix, M., Hoffmann, J. and Sempels, C. (2010), 'Le marketing dans l'économie de la connaissance : apports et implications de la cocréation de valeur', in Dibiaggio, L. and Meschi, P.-X. (eds), *Le management dans l'économie de la connaissance : des clés pour comprendre les nouveaux modèles.* Paris: Pearson Edition.

29 Fashion Mag (2011), La Chine deviendrait le premier marché mondial du luxe d'ici à 2020 : article based on a Crédit Lyonnais Securities Asia (CLSA) report.

30 Fashion Mag (2011), L'Inde fait rêver le luxe, http://fr. fashionmag.com/news-164340-L-Inde-fait-rever-le-luxe retrieved 12 May 2011.

31 Source: www.domrestaurante.com.br/#/en-us/sobre retrieved 12 May 2011.

32 China Daily (2011), Chanel Builds a New Channel in China, source: http://europe.chinadaily.com.cn/epaper/2011-02/11/ content_11984506.htm retrieved 12 May 2011.

33 Shanghai Tang Corporate website from http://www. shanghaitang.com/ shanghaitang-modern-chinese-chic-ambassador retrieved 25 April 2011.

CHAPTER 5

1 Chevalier, M. and Mazzalovo, G. (2008), *Luxury Brand Management: A World of Privilege*, Singapore, John Wiley & Sons, pp. 374–379.

2 Chevalier, M. and Mazzalovo, G. (2008), op. cit., pp. 345–346.

3 McKinsey & Company (2010), *Digital Nation on the Rise: Profiting from China's Internet Revolution* (2010 Annual Chinese Consumer Study), www.mckinsey.com; Value Partners (2010), *Luxury 2.0: The Role of Digital Channels in a Downturn,* retrieved 23 May 2011 from http://www.valuepartners.com/VP_pubbl_pdf/PDF_ Comunicati/Perspective//2009/Value-partners-Luxury-2.0-Marone-Chua.pdf.

4 Kapferer, J. N. and Bastien V. (2009), 'The specificity of luxury management: Turning marketing upside down', *Journal of Brand Management*, 16, 5–6, pp. 311–322.

5 Okonkwo, U. (2009), 'Sustaining the luxury brand on the Internet', *Journal of Brand Management*, 16, 5–6, pp. 302–310.

6 Idem.

7 Chaddah, R. and Husband, P. (2006), *The Cult of the Luxury Brand*, Boston, Nicholas Brealey International, pp. 284–285.

8 Okonkwo, U. (2009), op. cit.

9 Dubois, B., Laurent, G. and Czellar, S. (2001), 'Consumer Relationship to luxury: Analyzing complex and ambivalent attitudes', *HEC Paris Research paper*, 1 October.

10 Idem.

11 Dubois, B. and Paternault, C. (1995), 'Understanding the world of international luxury brands', *Journal of Advertising Research*, 1, pp. 273–278.

12 Okonkwo, U. (2009), op. cit.

13 Chevalier, M. and Mazzalovo, G. (2008), op. cit.

14 Kapferer, J. N. and Bastien, V. (2009), *The Luxury Strategy: Break the Rules of Marketing to Build Luxury Brands*, London, Kogan Page, p. 199.

15 Okonkwo, U. (2010), *Luxury Online*, London, Palgrave Macmillan, pp. 121, 156–161, 231–251.

16 Tungate, M., *Luxury World*, London, Kogan Page, pp.51–56, 123–129.

17 Kapferer, J. N. and Bastien, V. (2009), op. cit., pp. 194, 197, 199.

18 Kapferer, J. N. and Bastien, V. (2009), op. cit., p. 204.

19 Dunne, P. M., Lusch, R. F. and Carver, J. R. (2010), *Retailing*, South Western College, pp. 488–496.

20 Kapferer, J. N. and Bastien, V. (2009), op. cit., p. 68.

21 Okonkwo, U. (2007) *Luxury Fashion Branding,* London, Palgrave Macmillan, pp. 78–93.

22 Okonkwo, U. (2010), op. cit., pp. 156–161.

23 Okonkwo, U. (2007), op. cit., pp. 126–127.

24 Idem., p. 162.

25 Idem., p. 132.

26 www.digiscents.com.

27 Okonkwo, U. (2007), op. cit., pp. 144–145.

28 Azuma, R. (1997), 'A Survey of Augmented Reality Presence: Teleoperators and Virtual Environments', *Presence: Teleoperators and Virtual Environments,* 6, 4, pp. 355–385.

29 Chevalier, M. and Mazzalovo, G. (2008), op. cit., p. 349.

30 Sacerdote, E. (2007), *La Strategia Retail nella Modal e nel Lusso,* Milano, Franco Angeli, pp. 99–100.

31 Luxury Daily (2011) Bulgari breaks into Facebook commerce via Enchanted Garden app. Retrieved 23May 2011 from http://www.luxurydaily.com/bulgari-breaks-into-facebook-commerce-via-enchanted-garden-app/

32 Kapferer, J. N. and Bastien, V. (2009), op. cit., p. 189.

33 Luxury Daily (2011), *Yves Saint Laurent opens store on Cosmopolitan Boulevard.* Retrieved 21 March from http://www.luxurydaily.com/yves-saint-laurent-opens-store-on-cosmopolitan-boulevard/

34 BBC News (2009), *Fabergé Looks to Reinvent Itself Online.* Retrieved 28 September from http://news.bbc.co.uk/1/hi/business/8255647.stm

35 Idem.

36 http://news.bbc.co.uk/1/hi/business/8255647.stm, www.ibm.com. *Fabergé pushes boundaries to deliver luxury shopping experience on the Web.* Retrieved from http://www-304.ibm.com/easyaccess/fileserve?contentid=186081

37 Sacerdote, E. (2007), op. cit., pp. 172–175.

38 Idem.

39 Idem.

40 GMT Magazine (2010), *Boutiques Experience Dizzying Change.* Retrieved from http://www.gmtmag.com/en/22_fin_boutiques.php.

41 Luxury Daily (2011) *Harrods, Nordstrom on Same Page: In-store, Online Consistency Key*. Retrieved 22March 2011 from http://www.luxurydaily.com/the-importance-and-benefits-of-maintaining-online-and-in-store-consistency/

42 Idem.

43 Bonvin, S. (2 November 2009), 'Gilles Lipovetsky et le luxe émotionnel', *Le Temps*, p. 26.

CHAPTER 6

1 *Yahoo! Search Academy* (2010), Retrieved 10 March 2010 from http://www.flickr.com/photos/yahoo_presse/4477558968/in/photostream/

2 Xerfi Group (2010), *The Precepta Study 'The Luxury Groups' Internet strategies'*, Retrieved January 2010 from http://www.xerfi.fr/etudes/9DIS46.pdf

3 *Orient-Express Hotels, Trains and Cruises Ltd* (2010 data). Official company website, Retrieved from http://www.orient-express.com.

4 Benchmark Group, *Journal du net* (2010), web article 'Les usages du Web par les internautes', Retrieved 5 Octobre 2010 from http://www.journaldunet.com/cc/01_internautes/inter_usage_fr.shtml.

5 Benchmark Group, *Journal du Net* (2008), Interview of Boucheron's CEO J.C Bédos, Retrieved 5 March 2008 from http://www.journaldunet.com/ebusiness/commerce/interview/jean-christophe-bedos-boucheron-sur-internet-nous-sommes-condamnes-a-l-excellence.shtml.

6 *Altimeter Group*. Official company website, Retrieved from http://www.altimetergroup.com.

7 *The Financial Times* (2010), 'Facebook becomes bigger hit than Google' by C. Nuttall and D. Gelles, Retrieved 16 March 2010 from http://www.ft.com/cms/s/2/67e89ae8-30f7-11df-b057-00144feabdc0.html#axzz17pN3sCKa.

8 *Time* (2010), 'How Facebook is Redefining Privacy', by D. Fletcher, Retrieved 20 May 2010 from http://www.time.com/time/business/article/0,8599,1990582,00.html.

9 Ibid.

10 Facebook corporate website (2010), *Facebook's Press Center Statistics*, Retrieved from http://www.facebook.com/press/info.php?statistics.

11 Ibid.

CHAPTER 7

1 Sicard, M.-C. (2006), *Luxe, mensonges et marketing mais que font les marques de luxe?* Paris: Pearson Education France.

2 Bastien, V. and Kapferer, J.-N. (2008), *Luxe oblige*, Paris: Groupe Eyrolles.

3 Alleres, D. (2006), *Luxe métiers et management atypiques*, Paris: Economica.

4 Bronner, J.-C., Reigninger, C., Rouget, M., Tapies, J., Daumas, J.-C., De Ferrière Le Vayer, M. and Béjean, M. (2007), Le luxe aujourd'hui, *Entreprise et Histoire*, 46, pp. 177–187.

5 Chevalier, M. and Mazzalovo, G. (2008), *Luxury Brand Management a World of Privilege*, Singapore: John Wiley and Sons Asia Pte. Ltd.

6 Fionda, A., and Moore, C. (2009), The anatomy of a luxury fashion brand, *Journal of Brand Management*, 16 (5/6), pp. 347–363.

7 Kapferer, J.-N. (2008), *The New Strategic Brand Management Creating and Sustaining Brand Equity Long Term*, London: Kogan Page Limited.

8 Kapferer, J.-N. (2008), op. cit.

9 Sicard, M.-C. (2006), op. cit.

10 Kapferer, J.-N. (2007), *Les marques capital de l'entreprise*, Paris: Groupe Eyrolles, p. 98.

11 Kapferer, J.-N. (2008), op. cit.

12 Sicard, M.-C. (2006), op. cit.

13 Okonkwo, U. (2007), *Luxury Fashion Branding Trends, Tactics and Techniques*, New York: Palgrave Macmillan.

14 Keller, K. L. (2009), Managing the growth tradeoff challenges and opportunities in luxury branding, *Journal of Brand Management*, 16 (5/6), pp. 290–301.

15 Okonkwo, U. (2007), op. cit.

16 Sicard, M.-C. (2006), op. cit.

17 Okonkwo, U. (2007), op. cit.

18 Ibid.

19 Ibid.

20 Ibid.

21 Chevalier, M. and Mazzalovo, G. (2008), op. cit.

22 Okonkwo, U. (2007), op. cit.

23 Ballantyne, R., Warren, A. and Nobbs, K. (2006), The evolution of brand choice, *Journal of Brand Management*, 13 (4/5), pp. 339–352.

24 Okonkwo, U. (2007), op. cit.

25 Keller, K. L. (2009), op. cit.

26 Okonkwo, U. (2007), op. cit.

27 Okonkwo, U. (2007), op. cit.

28 Ibid., p. 114.

29 Bastien, V. and Kapferer, J.-N. (2008), op. cit.

30 Chevalier, M. and Mazzalovo, G. (2008), op. cit.

31 Clifton, R. (2009), *Brand and Branding*, London: The Economist/Profile Books Ltd.

32 Keller, K. L. (2008), *Strategic Brand Management Building, Measuring and Managing Brand Equity*, Upper Saddle River: Pearson Education.

33 Okonkwo, U. (2007), op. cit.

34 Riezebos, R. (2003), *Brand Management: A Theoretical and Practical Approach*. Harlow: Financial Times/Prentice Hall.

35 Kapferer, J.-N. and Bastien, V. (2009), The specificity of luxury management turning marketing upside down, *Journal of Brand Management*, 16 (5/6), pp. 311–322, 316.

36 Okonkwo, U. (2007), op. cit.

37 Ibid.

38 Sicard, M.-C. (2006), op. cit.

39 Okonkwo, U. (2007), op. cit.

40 Fionda, A. and Moore, C. (2009), op. cit.

41 Mikolajczak, C. (29 November 2007), Delvaux commercial dans le sens noble du terme, *La Libre Belgique*.

42 Chevalier, M. and Mazzalovo, G. (2008), op. cit.

43 Tungate, M. (2008), *Fashion Branding Style from Armani to Zara*, London: Kogan Page.

44 Fionda, A. and Moore, C. (2009), op. cit.

45 Alleres, D. (1999), 'The behaviour of the young towards luxury products', in Antonides, G. and van Raaij, W. F. (eds) *Cases in Consumer Behavior*, West Sussex: John Wiley and Sons.

46 Fionda, A. and Moore, C. (2009), op. cit.

47 Ibid.

48 Lewi, G. and Lacoeuilhe, J. (2007), *Branding Management: la marque de l'idée à l'action,* Paris: Pearson Education.

49 Kapferer, J.-N. and Bastien, V. (2009), op. cit.

50 Berthon, P., Pitt, L., Parent, M. and Berthon, J. P. (2009), Aesthetics and ephemerality: Observing and preserving the luxury brand, *California Review of Management*, 52 (1), pp. 45–66.

51 Chevalier, M. and Mazzalovo, G. (2008), op. cit.

52 Fionda, A. and Moore, C. (2009), op. cit.; Tungate, M. (2008), op. cit.

53 Berg, J. (2004), Should a luxury leather goods brand diversify into ready-to-wear? *Journal du Textile*, retrieved 15 August 2005 from http://www.estin.com/publications/pdf/luxury_leather_eng.pdf.

54 Sicard, M.-C. (2006), op. cit.

55 Fionda, A. and Moore, C. (2009), op. cit.

56 Dereumaux, R. M. (2007), Le luxe et l'image de marque, *Market Management,* 1 (5), pp. 70–78.

57 Sicard, M.-C. (2006), op. cit.

58 Fionda, A. and Moore, C. (2009), op. cit.; Kapferer, J.-N. (2007), op. cit.; Keller, K. L. (2009), op. cit.

59 Chevalier, M. and Mazzalovo, G. (2008), op. cit.

60 Fionda, A. and Moore, C. (2009), op. cit.

61 Sicard, M.-C. (2006), op. cit.

62 Catry, B. (2007), Le luxe peut être chère mais est-il toujours rare? *Revue Française de Gestion,* 171, pp. 49–63.

63 Pau, I. and Pendergast, G. (2000), Consuming luxury brands the relevance of the rarity principle, *Journal of Brand Management*, 8 (2), pp. 122–138.

64 Okonkwo, U. (2007), op. cit.

65 Fionda, A. and Moore, C. (2009), op. cit.

66 Sicard, M.-C. (2006), op. cit.

67 Tungate, M. (2008), op. cit.

68 Degoutte, C. (2007), Stratégie de marques dans la mode: convergence ou divergence des modèles de gestion nationaux dans l'industrie du luxe (1860-2003)?, *Entreprise et Histoire,* 46, pp. 125–142.

69 Diamond, E. (2006), *Fashion Retailing a Multichannel Approach,* New Jersey: Pearson Education.

70 Sicard, M.-C. (2006), op. cit.

71 Lewi, G. and Lacoeuilhe, J. (2007), op. cit.

72 Keller, K. L. (2009), op. cit.

73 Kapferer, J.-N. (2007), op. cit.

74 Zargani, L. (12 november 2007), Bottega Veneta's new Rome Home, *WWD*, 193 (30), p. 22.

75 Okonkwo, U. (2007), op. cit.

76 Fionda, A. and Moore, C. (2009), op. cit.

77 Clifton, R. (2009), op. cit.

78 Fionda, A. and Moore, C. (2009), op. cit.

79 Hatch, M. J. and Rubin, J. (2006), The hermeneutics of branding, *Journal of Brand Management*, 14, pp. 40–59.

CHAPTER 8

1 Aaker, D. A. (1991), *Managing Brand Equity*, New York: The Free Press.

2 Kapferer, J. N. (2008), *The New Strategic Brand Management: Creating and Sustaining Brand Equity Long Term,* 4th ed., Bodmin, Cornwall: MPG Books Ltd.

3 Best, R. J. (2009), *Market-based Management: Strategies for Growing Customer Value and Profitability,* 5th ed., Upper Saddle River, NJ: Pearson Prentice Hall.

4 Keller, K. L. (2003), *Strategic Brand Management: Building, Measuring, and Managing Brand Equity,* 2nd ed., Upper Saddle River, NJ: Pearson Education Ltd.

5 Kapferer, J. N. (2008), op. cit.

6 Czellar, S. (2003), Consumer attitude toward brand extensions: An integrative model and research propositions, *International Journal of Research in Marketing*, 20(1), 97–115.

7 Reddy, M., Terblanche, N., Pitt, L. and Parent, M. (2009), 'How far can luxury brands travel? Avoiding the pitfalls of luxury brand extension', *Business Horizons*, 52 (1), pp. 187–197.

8 Rolls-Royce: Keep on rolling, *The Economist*, retrieved 7 May 2009 from www.economist.com.

9 'Rolls-Royce Announces Record 2010 Sales', retrieved 10 January 2011 from www.rolls-roycemotorcars.com.

10 Aaker, D. A. (1991), op. cit.

11 Degen, Matt (2010), Test drive: 'Affordable' Rolls-Royce Ghost, *The Orange County Register* (18/02/10).

12 Ford, T. (2010) Rolls-Royce Ghost: super natural. Topgear.com site. http://www.topgear.com/uk/photos/rolls-ghost-super-natural

13 Keller, K. L. (2003), op. cit.

14 Aaker, D. A. (1991), op. cit.

15 Kapferer, J. N. (2008), op. cit.

16 Kapferer, J. N. and Bastien, V. (2009), *The Luxury Strategy: Break the Rules of Marketing to Build Strong Brands*, London & Philadelphia: Kogan Page Ltd.

17 *Mercedes-Benz Annual Report 1998.*

18 *Mercedes-Benz Annual Report 1999.*

19 Maynard, Shawn (2004), Mercedes-Benz Recalls 680,000 Cars for Sensotronic Braking System, *Automobile.com.*

20 Mackintosh, J. and Milne, R. (2005), Electronic bugs cause recall of 1.3m cars by Mercedes, *Financial Times,* retrieved 01 April 2011 from www.ft.com.

21 Kapferer, J. N. and Bastien, V. (2009), op. cit.

22 Luxury Institute European Survey – Wealthy European Consumers Rate the Most Prestigious Auto Brands: Porsche, Mercedes-Benz, and Jaguar. Marketwire.com site (9 Sep, 2008). http://www.marketwire.com/press-release/luxury-institute-european-survey-wealthy-european-consumers-rate-most-prestigious-auto-897988.htm

23 *Armani Annual Report 2009.*

24 Swengley, N. (2004), And beware of a drive for quick profits – it can lead to over-exposure of a brand, *Financial Times*, retrieved 01 April 2011 from www.ft.com.

25 The dangers of value ranges, *Financial Times*, retrieved 15 March 2009 from www.ft.com/cms/s/0/240b1a5c-1312-11de-a170-00 00779fd2ac.html.

26 Kapferer, J. N. and Bastien, V. (2009), op. cit.

27 Keller, K. L. (2003), op. cit.

28 *Interbrand Best Global Brands report 2009.*

29 Roe, L. (2007), Mi Casa Su Casa. *Vogue UK*, retrieved 01 April 2011 from http://www.vogue.co.uk/news/daily/2007-04/ 070418-mi-casa-su-casa.aspx.

30 Sherman, L. (2009), World's Most Powerful Luxury Brands, *Forbes,* retrieved 1 May 2009 from www.forbes.com/2009/05/ 01/powerful-luxury-brands-lifestyle-style-luxury-brands. html.

31 Jimmy Choo for H&M (2009), *Telegraph.co.uk,* retrieved 01 April 2011 from http://fashion.telegraph.co.uk/columns/hilary-alexander/TMG5560221/Jimmy-Choo-for-HandM.html.

32 Is Luxury Brand Missoni Next in Line to Launch H&M Collection? (2009) *Famespy.com,* retrieved 14 May 2009 from http://famespy. com/2009/05/14/is-luxury-brand-missoni-next-in-line-to-launch-hm-collection/.

33 Aaker, D. A. (1991), op. cit.

34 Valter, V. (2009), Jimmy Choo plus Hunter, *Millionlooks.com*, retrieved 01 April 2011 from www.millionlooks.com/footwear/ jimmy-choo-plus-hunter/

35 Friedman, V. (2010), 'Lunch with the FT: Tamara Mellon', *Ft.com,* retrieved 04 December 2010 from www.ft.com/cms/s/2/ 9d821ce2-fe60-11df-845b-00144feab49a.html#axzz183IuLExR.

36 Apparel, Accessories & Luxury Goods Industry Profile: Global, *Datamonitor*, March 2010.

37 Silverstine, M. J. and Fiske, N. (2005), *Trading Up*, New York: Penguin Group.

38 Roberts, A. (2010), Now the Kids Can Wear Designer Outfits, *Business Week*, retrieved 16 September 2010 from www. businessweek.com.

39 Ibid.

40 De Mesa, A. (2004), Born into luxury, *Brandchannel.com,* retrieved 01 April 2011 from http://www.brandchannel.com/features_ effect.asp?pf_id= 230.

41 Peck, S. (2010), Luxury Clothes For Kids, *Forbes,* retrieved 13 July 2010 from http://www.forbes.com/2010/07/13/luxury-clothing-kids-lifestyle-style-fashion.html.

42 Kotler, P. and Keller, K. L. (2006), *Marketing Management,* 12th ed., Upper Saddle River, NJ: Pearson Education Ltd.

43 White, B. (2010), Stella McCartney Kids Preview, *Telegraph.co.uk,* retrieved 03 November 2010 from http://fashion.telegraph.co. uk/columns/belinda-white/TMG8106917/Stella-McCartney-Kids-preview.html.

44 Abraham, T. (2010), Eat your heart out Suri Cruise! How Gucci and Stella McCartney are targeting future fashionistas with designer childrenswear, *Daulymail.co.uk,* retrieved 06 November 2010 from www.dailymail.co.uk/femail/article-1326634/Gucci-Stella-McCartneys-designer-childrenswear-Eat-heart-Suri-Cruise. html.

CHAPTER 9

1 http://www.ifop.com/media/pressdocument/205-2-document_ file.pdf.

2 Bendell J. and Kleanthous A. (2007), Deeper Luxury, a report from WWF-UK.

3 Drennan K. (2010), Sustainable luxury: an emerging trend?, http://ecosalon.com/sustainable-luxury-an-emerging-trend/

4 Bendell J. and Kleanthous A. (2007), op. cit.

5 Ray P. H. and Anderson S. R. (2000), *The Cultural Creatives,* New York: Harmony Books.

6 Association for Cultural Biodiversity (2007), *Les créatifs culturels en France* (Cultural creatives in France), Gap: Yves Michel Editions.

7 http://www.guardian.co.uk/sustainable-business/ sustainable-luxury-fashion-growth-shoppers.

8 http://www.bbc.co.uk/news/world-europe-12021328.

9 Bendell J. and Kleanthous A. (2007), op. cit.

10 http://www.ifop.com/media/pressdocument/205-2-document_file.pdf.

11 'Twelve rules for the 21st century luxury enterprise', a white paper from the Luxury Institute (July 2009), http://static.luxurysociety.com/download/LuxuryInstitute-21stCenturyLuxuryEnterprise-2009.pdf.

12 http://www.lohas.com/content/how-lohas-changing-business-asia.

13 Bendell J. and Kleanthous A. (2007), op. cit., p. 14.

14 http://www.sustainabilitycentre.com.au/SD_China2.pdf.

15 http://www.ifop.com/media/poll/dirigeantsetecologie.pdf.

16 Ifop Survey for the Group 'La Poste' on the attitudes of big companies regarding sustainable development, conducted in March 2009.

17 www.footprintnetwork.org/en/index.php/GFN/page/earth_overshoot_day/#WOD.

18 http://oilprice.com/Energy/Crude-Oil/Dramatic-Shift-in-the-Peak-Oil-Debate.html.

19 Bourg D. and Whiteside K. (2010), *Vers une démocratie écologique*, Paris: Seuil Editions.

20 www.telegraph.co.uk/finance/newsbysector/industry/mining/6546579/Barrick-shuts-hedge-book-as-world-gold-supply-runs-out.html.

21 Information Office of the State Council, People's Repubilc of China, 2003. La politique de la Chine en matière de ressources minérales, http://french.china.org.cn/fa-book/f_kuang/xinjiang-s.htm.

22 Bendell J. and Kleanthous A.(2007), op. cit., p. 9.

23 For example http://www.greenpeace.org/raw/content/seasia/en/press/reports/cyanide-gold-mining-s-devasta.pdf.

24 http://www.business-humanrights.org/Categories/Sectors/
Naturalresources/Mining.

25 http://www.peta.org/action/rather-go-naked.aspx.

26 For example www.ecorazzi.com, the most well-known ecorazzi
website, with more than 500,000 visits per month.

27 Sempels C. and Vandercammen M. (2009), *Oser le marketing
durable*, Paris: Pearson Editions.

28 Schwesinger Berlie L. (2009), *Alliances for Sustainable
Development: Business and NGO Partnerships*, Hampshire: Palgrave
Macmillan Editions; Hart S. L. and Sharma S. (2004), 'Engaging
fringe stakeholders for competitive imagination', *Academy of
Management Executive*, 19, 1, 7–18; Jamali D. and
Keshishian T. (2009), 'Uneasy alliances: lessons learned from
partnership between businesses and NGOs in the context of CSR',
Journal of Business Ethics, 84, 2, 277–295. (non exhaustive list).

29 Schwesinger Berlie L. (2009), op. cit.; Verger O. and
White G. (2004), 'Les partenariats entreprises-ONG dans le cadre
de démarches sociétales' Report from IMS Entreprendre pour la
Cité.

30 See Schwesinger Berlie L. (2009), op. cit., for a deep review.

31 http://www.ellenmacarthurfoundation.org/convince_me – The
Big Idea video.

32 Schmidheiny S. (1992), *Changing Course: A Global Business
Perspective on Development and the Environment*, Cambridge, MA:
The MIT Press (a publication from the World Business Council of
Sustainable Development).

33 Klostermann J. E. M. and Tukker A. (2010), *Product Innovation and
Eco-Efficiency: Twenty-Two Industry Efforts to Reach the Factor 4*,
New-York, USA: Springer.

34 LVMH 2009 report on 'Preserving the Environment', http://www.
lvmh.com/groupe/Donnee_env_2009_gbr.pdf.

35 Decrease related to the eco-redesign of the packaging, but also
because of a decline in the activity.

36 http://www.biomimicryinstitute.org/

37 Fletcher K. (2007), *Sustainable Fashion and Textiles: Design Journeys*, London: Earthscan Ltd.

38 http://www.biomimicryinstitute.org/home-page-content/home-page-content/biomimicking-sharks.html.

39 Benyus J. M. (2002), *Biomimicry: Innovation Inspired by Nature*, New York: Harper Perennial; Rouer M. and Gouyon A. (2007), *Réparer la planète: la révolution de l'économie positive*, Jean-Claude Lattès & BeCitizen Editions (co-edition).

40 http://www.biomimicryinstitute.org/about-us/biomimicry-a-tool-for-innovation.html

41 http://www.whirlpool.fr/app.cnt/whr/fr_BE/pageid/pgwpdswstn grnhome001

42 For example Sempels C. and Vandercammen M. (2009), op. cit.; Stahel, W. R. (2000), From products to services: selling performance instead of goods, www.greeneconomics.net/Stahel%20Essay1.doc; Bourg D. and Buclet N. (2005), 'L'économie de la fonctionnalité: changer la consommation dans le sens du développement durable', *Futuribles*, 313 (November), 27–37.

43 Bendell J. and Kleanthous A. (2007), op. cit.

44 'Wealth and Luxury trends 2011 and beyond', a report from the Luxury Institute, October 2010, http://www.luxuryinstitute.com/Documents/LuxuryInstitute-WhitePaper-Trendsfor2011.pdf.

45 Neely A. (2009), 'Exploring the financial consequences of the servitization of manufacturing' *Operations Management Research*, 1, 2, 103–118.

46 http://www.bagborroworsteal.com/welcome; http://luxuryhandbaghire.co.uk/

47 Example based on Combe, V., Perrier, S., Pireyn, B., and Richard, C. (2008), 'Etude prospective sur l'économie de la fonctionnalité en France', http://www.inspire-institut.org/etude-prospective-sur-leconomie-de-fonctionnalite-en-france.html.

48 http://www.fondationentreprisehermes.org.

49 http://en.wikipedia.org/wiki/Water_hyacinth.

50 http://www.unicef.org/corporate_partners/index_40631.html.

INDEX